EVILLE-BUNCOMBE TECHNICAL INSTITUTE NORTH CAROLINA
STATE BOARD OF EDUCATION
DEPT. OF COMMUNITY COLLEGES
LIBRARIES

# *Handbook of Practical Boat Repairs*

DISCARDED

APR 2 4 2025

D1523420

*About the Author*

Percy W. Blandford has had a lifelong interest in boats of all types. He built his first craft—a canvas-covered canoe—in 1930, and hasn't been without a boat since. He has personally built more than 100 boats, ranging from dinghies to sailing and power cruisers; and he is a seasoned seaman, having sailed in and around Europe and North America.

He writes from personal experience, having repaired or supervised the repair of countless craft and their associated equipment. A practical craftsman, he can rightfully claim to be one of the few naval architects to personally build many prototypes of his own design—many of which are in practical operation the world over.

For the past 25 years he has been designing boats, specializing in smaller craft, or writing about them—producing a staggering proliferation of 47 books and over 3000 articles. Blandford's wider interests include travel and craftsmanship in its many forms. He is also an accomplished photographer and has an uncanny ability as an author/draftsman: all the photographs and line drawings in this book are his own.

# Handbook
# of Practical
# Boat Repairs

## By Percy W. Blandford

**TAB BOOKS**
Blue Ridge Summit, Pa. 17214

FIRST EDITION

FIRST PRINTING— AUGUST 1975

Copyright © 1975 by TAB BOOKS

Printed in the United States
of America

Reproduction or publication of the content in any manner. without express permission of the publisher. is prohibited. No liability is assumed with respect to the use of the information herein.

Hardbound Edition: International Standard Book No. 0-8306-5788-6

Paperbound Edition: International Standard Book No. 0-8306-4788-0

Library of Congress Card Number: 75-13010

# *Preface*

Some yachtsmen only enjoy their craft by using them. When they are not sailing, fishing, motorboating, paddling, or rowing, they would rather have someone else look after their boats. Other yachtsmen get as much pleasure taking care of their craft as they do using them; they get considerable satisfaction out of maintaining their boats, making improvements, or doing repair work. In these days of mass production, not so many people get an opportunity to see a job done right. The man who works on his boat gets an opportunity to savor the feeling of a job well done. The man who pays someone else to do the job, on the other hand, misses this increasingly rare feeling of satisfaction.

In general, what the professional can offer in skill can be balanced by what the amateur has available in almost unlimited quantities: time. If you have a capacity for doing careful work, you can usually achieve professional results—it will just take you longer than it would the expert. Time means money to the professional; to the amateur, it can mean more enjoyment of his hobby and the satisfaction of seeing a practical task done well—something denied many of us in our everyday work. There is also the satisfaction of saving money.

Of course, few repairs can be made without tools. What is possible in the way of owner maintenance depends on the kit of tools kept available. When assessing a repair job, a decision about the need for heavy equipment or professional help will have to be made. However, it is often possible to fabricate parts, having only to call in expert help with tasks of such magnitude as to be beyond the capabilities of an amateur.

This book is an attempt to comprehensively cover all the repair work an amateur might consider tackling, not only to the boat itself, but to all the equipment, fittings, and accessories that make the rather complex whole that is a present-day sailor's property—whether a modest canoe, dinghy, outboard motorboat, or a more ambitious sailing or power cabin boat.

The emphasis is on practical ideas. There are many techniques and improvisations little known outside boatyards that are included herein. I believe that this book contains far more practical information on all aspects of boat repair than has been gathered in one volume before. It is the outcome of a lifetime of doing practical jobs whenever possible. I hope that it will be of value to the large numbers of boat owners who are looking for guidance with boat repair problems. With the book beside you, suitable tools and materials at hand, and enough patience, almost anything is possible.

It is impossible to acknowledge all the help given in supplying information for the compilation of this book. Most of the content is based on my own experience, but many people, thankfully, allowed themselves to be photographed at work. I am especially thankful to the Samson Cordage Company of Boston, Massachusetts for information on methods of splicing braided cordage.

Percy W. Blandford

# Contents

# Repair Supplies

You may hope that damage never occurs to your boat. You may hope that any accidents that happen will involve the other fellow's craft. Unfortunately, hope is not enough. One of the attributes of a true seaman is that he does all he can to avoid accidents; but if they do occur, he knows what to do. In an emergency at sea you have to depend entirely on your own resources; much more so than in a comparable emergency ashore. If your car breaks down, it is unlikely that you will suffer more than inconvenience. But if your boat breaks down, springs a leak, or is otherwise incapacitated at sea, you could suffer anything, including loss of life.

## FIRST-AID SUPPLIES

One of the most useful things to appear on the boating scene in recent years is waterproof adhesive tape. It is available in rolls of various widths and often comes in different colors. Some of it is sold as electrician's tape. Some of it has nonboating applications, such as in forming the white lines on a wooden floor for a game area. Tapes with fabric embedded in the plastic are strong and particularly useful for boat repair.

The most generally useful tape width is 2 in. If greater width is needed, strips of tape can be overlapped. The tape will adhere with hand pressure to almost any material—rigid or flexible—but it grips best to a smooth surface rather than anything uneven. Because the adhesive is waterproof, it will not stick to a damp surface; any attempt to use the tape over moisture will be unsuccessful. Rubbing the damp surface with a cloth dipped in alcohol immediately before pressing the tape into place will usually overcome this problem, however.

The tape has two main purposes: keeping water out and strengthening a weakened part. I have seen a good example of its waterproofing ability; a sailing dinghy had a 6 in. hole knocked out of its side near the waterline by another boat. A piece of cardboard was cut to cover the hole and fixed in place with overlapping layers of 2 in. plastic tape. The boat sailed on for several hours. The cardboard was used to provide stiffness over the comparatively large area. For a smaller hole, tape alone would have been sufficient.

The tape's ability to strengthen a weakened part became evident when a boathook was used to pry a boat away from a dock. There was an ominous creaking as wood began to split. The cracked part was bound with tape and the operation continued without mishap.

Other comparatively new things of value for use on board are waterproof sealing compounds. Usually sold in tubes, they never completely harden. They are of several different chemical compositions, but for emergency use on a boat almost any of them would be suitable. Even one intended for bathroom use might do, but it is better to get a boating type from a marine supplier. Like waterproof adhesive tape, these compounds adhere to almost any dry surface. In an emergency you may have to dry a crack near the surface only and rely on the compound holding there; but later it would be advisable to remove the compound and dry out any moisture trapped below the surface. Harder compounds of the plastic-wood type are not much use for minor emergency repairs, although they can be used in holes where screws have worked loose.

Carry a few feet of copper wire. Copper is more ductile than other metals and can be twisted by hand or with pliers to lock such things as shackles that persistently loosen. However, there is not much strength in copper wire; where a load has to be taken, galvanized-iron wire is better. Several turns of iron wire, with the ends twisted tightly, may do temporary duty in place of a shackle.

What to carry for first-aid repairs to machinery depends on the engine. For the outboard motor the most likely supplies are spare plugs and the tools to change them. If the motor transmits power through a shear pin, there should be several spares and the tools to deal with them.

## IN-SEASON MAINTENANCE

Minor repairs and routine maintenance overlap, particularly during the season when boats get frequent use. If there is a difference, it is that *maintenance* is the work done to keep the boat in a state where repairs should not be needed; *repairs* are called for when something unforeseen has to be dealt with. Maintenance may be described as preventive repair.

Rope can suffer during a season of use. Watch for fraying ends or chafing where the rope passes through chocks or over dock edges. Rubber or plastic rubing slipped over rope dock lines will protect them (Fig. 1-1). If it cannot be slipped over, it may be split down one side and sprung over, then held in place with waterproof tape. There should be a reel or ball of *whipping* (stitching) line on board to replace any that shows signs of fraying. Modern synthetic-fiber rope will quickly unravel and be wasted if not sealed or whipped at the end.

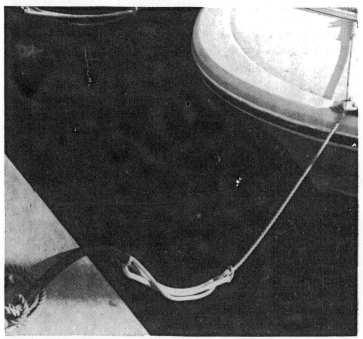

Fig. 1-1. A dock line protected from chafing with a piece of rubber tubing. A rubber "snubber" in the line relieves the shock of a surging boat.

Most boatbuilding materials have to be protected by paint. If wood is rubbed bare, it will absorb water and appear permanently dirty. If the original finish was clear varnish, the dirt will show through no matter how much it is later rubbed down in preparation for varnishing. Bare steel will rust where rubbed bare, as will ferroconcrete when it absorbs moisture. Unprotected aluminum is less affected, and fiberglass in good condition can be left unpainted. But if the boat has been painted and a patch is rubbed bare, a touchup is advisable to preserve a consistent surface under the finish.

For a temporary touchup, any quick-setting paint may be used. A brush can be carried in a sealed container of solvent to insure its usefulness when the need arises; few things are more aggravating than having to do a paint job with a brush that might as well be a spatula. Aerosol paints can be used as an alternative to brushing, but the necessarily thin consistency of spray paints may mean applying several coats; one wipe of a brush with a thicker paint would be sufficient. Some paints do not adhere well to fiberglass, so an appropriate one should be carried.

Wood which has chafed may be rough to the touch. Quite often a knife blade held on edge can be used as a scraper to smooth down standing fibers. However, a medium grade of sandpaper (waterproof) will serve better in this respect, especially just prior to painting. Sandpaper is also useful for rubbing rust off steel or brightening brasswork.

Polishes of various sorts may be considered maintenance items rather than repair materials. Some polishes provide a limited amount of protection, particularly those that leave a wax deposit. However, polishing wood, metal, or fiberglass, acts as an incentive to get everything shipshape. Polishing may also show up minor blemishes that might not have been noticed otherwise.

## THE REPAIR KIT

The pioneer is supposed to have done everything with one tool: his axe—from building his home to sharpening a pencil, or even shaving. Primitive boatbuilders built their dugout craft with an adze-like tool and very little else. Some still do, but the tools of civilized society have reached just about everywhere in the world. Even if craftsmen with very limited equipment were able to achieve wonders, they might have done better with more sophisticated tools, and would certainly have consumed much less labor and time. It is the same with boat repairs. Providing there is sufficient skill, it may be possible to make a satisfactory job with very little equipment; but to deal properly with work about a boat, the more tools of the right sort available, the easier it will be to achieve a workmanlike result.

## BASIC TOOLS

That is not say it is necessary to spend a lot of money on a large selection of tools before embarking on repairs. It would certainly be unwise to buy a so-called kit of tools. Such a collection of tools assembled by someone else will almost certainly contain some things you may never use, and others which are the wrong size or otherwise unsuitable for your purpose. It is better to select individual tools to suit your individual needs and preferences.

Like most other things, the quality of a tool is usually related to its price, although bargains *are* sometimes obtainable. Secondhand tools can be quite a buy, providing you know what you are looking for. It is unwise to buy a cheap tool on the pretext that you will discard it when it wears out and replace it with another. Such tools, particularly those used to cut, may not work as well new as much-used, originally more expensive tools.

Most amateur handymen already have a number of tools that can be used for boat repairs. Anyone with craft experience may have preferences that differ from those set out here. In hand work, especially, there may be more than one way to do a job. An old-time professional would certainly look askance at the revolution that has come about with the introduction of small, electric hand tools. I remember my apprentice days and the disapproving comments that were made when I bought a steel plane. The craftsmen who were teaching me swore by their wooden ones.

Broadly speaking, the more tools you have, the more likely you will be to cope with any repair job that arises. However, this does not mean you should go out and buy all the tools you can afford. It is better to let your tool kit grow as you discover the need for certain items; that way, you will learn to appreciate the necessity of having the right tool for each particular job. To the uninitiated, a screwdriver is just a screwdriver; but in the maker's catalog there may be a hundred variations.

"Basic" is only a relative term as applied to a tool kit, but the tools suggested here are common to many repair jobs. The accompanying notes will offer guidance in selecting the first essential tools if you are starting from scratch.

## Screwdrivers

Screws come in many sizes, with heads of many shapes, and not always with the familiar slot. To do its job properly, the end of a screwdriver has to fit the screw. And not much tolerance can be allowed if the screw is to be driven or withdrawn without being damaged. If the screwdriver doesn't fit, it could slip off and damage the surrounding surface. Screw diameter is stated as a gage size, rather than a fractional measurement. A driver for a particular gage screw may suit a gage size bigger or smaller, but drivers and screws should not be interchanged among *types*.

For work on the average boat, three widths will deal with most screws. For ordinary slotted screw heads, the driver should present a straight, parallel end without rounded corners, so that it fits the slot easily and prevents slipping.

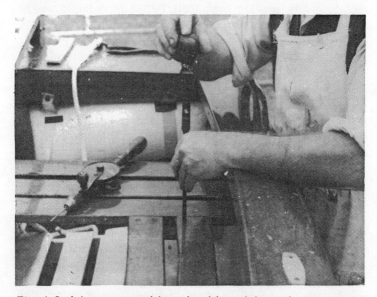

Fig. 1-2. A long screwdriver, besides giving a better reach can increase leverage.

Besides screwdrivers for slotted screws, it will be necessary to have others to fit special heads. The most common of these is the Phillips head. Instead of the slot, there is a star-shaped socket in the screw head. Phillips and other similar designs are really an aid in quantity production as they allow power driving, but the boat repairer will need only suitable screwdrivers. Fortunately, one or two Phillips sizes should suit all the screws found on a boat

Although it may not seem immediately obvious, more leverage can be applied with a long screwdriver than with a short one. (Fig. 1-2). The slight wobble from a direct thrust as the driver is turned helps to apply more torque. However, there is no need to go to extremes; there will be occasions when a very short screwdriver will have to be used to get into a confined space.

There are screwdrivers with replaceable and interchangeable points. These combination tools have their uses, particularly in a tool kit to be taken afloat. However, individual tools are probably slightly more effective and should be chosen if much work is anticipated, particularly ashore. Ratchet screwdrivers and pump-action drivers (Fig. 1-3) are useful when large numbers of screws need to be driven quickly in succession. If you have one already, it will obviously have its uses; but several plain screwdrivers bought for the cost of one special tool will be of more use in repair work.

Try the handles before buying screwdrivers. Not only should the handle be comfortable; it should allow you to exert a powerful twist. Smooth plastic may be comfortable, but it will not give you the tight grip of a wooden handle. A round handle may be easier to produce, and some grip may be provided by flutes, but the power you can exert will be greater with an oval handle. Needless to say, the handle should be secure. Look for looseness, especially in secondhand tools.

For most screws, sufficient leverage can be given with one hand on the handle. For large screws, there is an advantage in having a tool with a square shaft (smaller screwdrivers are mostly round) in that a wrench can be used to assist in turning. It is also worthwhile having a screwdriver bit that fits a carpenter's brace. The torque that can be applied is considerably more than by any hand method.

Differences between screwdrivers of different price, yet of comparable appearance, will almost certainly be due to

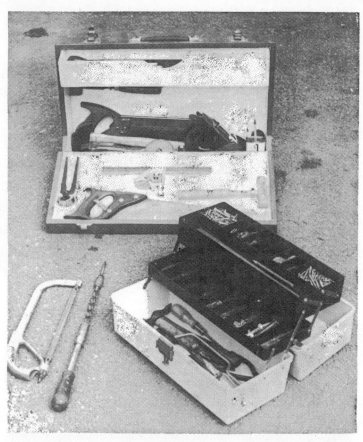

Fig. 1-3. The two loose tools are a pump-action screwdriver and a hacksaw with a storage space in the frame for blades.

differences in the quality and treatment of the steel used in the blade. The steel has to be hard enough to resist bending or the end in the screw slot buckling, yet it must not be so hard as to be brittle and break or crumble at the corners as it twists in the screw slot. These are the features you pay for. Stainless steel has not become common in screwdrivers, so be prepared to protect them from rust before they're taken afloat.

**Wrenches**

The infinite variety and sizes of wrenches reflect the inability of the engineering world to adopt standardization early enough in mechanical evolution to be truly effective. With international transport becoming easier and quicker, we find the products of many nations mixed with our own, so the standard screw systems of other countries have to be accommodated.

Adjustable wrenches will have to be included in the basic kit, but the jibe "knuckle-buster" indicates that such a wrench is not as good as a fixed one intended for the particular nut or bolt head.

In the long run it will probably be a good investment to buy a good-quality set of socket wrenches with interchangeable heads to suit several of the standard series of nuts. However, a good set is costly and at that won't guarantee you will not need other wrenches. For general purposes, open-ended wrenches are worth having. As the range of mechanical equipment that may have to be repaired is so great, it is probably as well to build up your wrench kit by buying at first to suit the job at hand. If you have to deal with electrical gear, a set of very small double-ended wrenches may be bought from an electrical goods dealer. For small nuts, the only tool that may reach into the close confines of electrical apparatus is a nutdriver. This looks like a screwdriver, but has an end to fit over the nut.

It would be unwise to accumulate a variety of special motor wrenches for other than superficial work until you know what you will have to deal with; in the meantime, use the tools provided by the engine manufacturer.

**Gripping Tools**

In boat repairs, more than in many other jobs, there is often a need to hold things in place or keep two parts together. The adage that the number of clamps you need is two more than you actually have has a lot of truth in it. Because of this, it is worthwhile getting together all the squeezing and gripping devices you can, whether they are designed as tools or are discarded parts of appliances. A few C-clamps, from about 4 inches upwards, should start the collection. A large clamp can usually be made to do the work of a small one with the aid of some packing.

Pliers are made in a large variety. They are for gripping small things and are *not substitutes* for wrenches or vises. Several combination types are available. These are satisfactory, providing the extra functions do not interfere with the main purpose. It is useful to have a built-in wire cutter and serrated hollows to grip small pipes and rods. Insulated

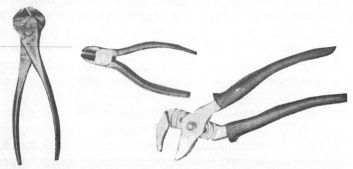

Fig. 1-4. From left to right: end or top cutters; side or angle cutters, both used for cutting wire or nails; pliers with adjustable pivot positions to allow a range of openings.

handles are often available. While it is unlikely that you will have to handle wires carrying high voltages, the insulation provides a better grip. Some pliers pivot in alternative positions—slip-joint and Channellock types—giving a choice of wide or narrow openings while allowing the jaws to remain parallel (See Fig. 1-4).

There are several plier-type tools which lock on to the work, either by a screw or lever action. In effect, they give you a third hand and may be regarded as small clamps. They are practically invaluable to have. There will be occasions when only long-nose or needle-nose pliers will fit the bill exactly. Round-nose pliers make neat wire loops. Thin-jawed pliers will get into restricted places. But all of these can be acquired later.

Pincers are allied to pliers, but have their own particular functions. They are only needed for removing nails. A broad base and long arms give the greatest leverage. Size is by length, 8—10 in. being usual. A pad will prevent damage to the surface. There should be sharp corners to the jaws so they can be dug into the wood, possibly with the help of a chisel cut to get under the nail head (Fig. 1-5).

## Hammers

The household hammer will probably serve for boat repairs, whatever its type. If one is bought, a head with a cross peen is more useful for boat work than the claw type. The cross peen gets into restricted places and is useful for riveting.

The claw hammer is more of a wrecking tool for rough carpentry. Avoid a hammer which is too heavy. If you find you

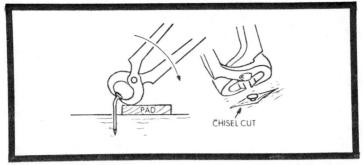

Fig. 1-5. Pincers are somewhat related to pliers, but are used to remove nails.

are sliding your hand towards the head instead of using the end of the handle, it is probably too heavy; 8–12 oz usually are the weights required, although one as light as 4 oz is useful for pins and tacks.

Traditionally, a steel hammer head was fitted to a wood (hickory or ash) handle by a waisted hole and wedge (Fig. 1-6A). Many more recent designs have the head and handle in one steel piece, with a rubber or plastic grip. This has the advantage of security, but the wood has the advantage of resilience to relieve the handle shock. Take your choice.

Engineers favor a ball peen hammer (Fig. 1-6B) which is used to spread rivet heads. There are other hammer heads, but since nearly all hitting will be done with the ordinary flat peen (actually slightly domed), it does not matter much what form the opposite side of the head of your first hammer takes.

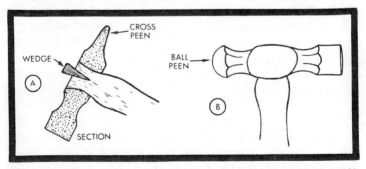

Fig. 1-6. The construction of the "traditional" hammer (A) and a ball peen hammer (B); although most work will be done with the flat peen, the round side is useful for spreading rivet heads.

19

Mallets are merely hammers with soft material for the head. Their special property is in giving a "soft" blow. If wood has to be driven into place, there is less risk of damage or splitting if a mallet is used instead of a hammer. When all chisel handles were wood, it was usual to hit them with a mallet; but the plastic used for the handles of most modern chisels can take a hammer blow without damage.

Allied to hammers are punches. A hammer blow may not fall exactly where you intended. A punch controls the point of impact, can get into places out of reach of the hammer, or drive a pin through a hole. It is worthwhile accumulating short pieces of rod of various diameters for use as punches, as well as punches per se. One or two center punches are useful for locating the start of drill holes in wood and metal.

**Hole-Making Tools**

In repair work, you will soon find a need to make holes in all sizes from $^1/_{16}$ inch up to 1 inch or more in wood, metal, or plastic. There are no alternatives to having the proper bits necessary for each size needed; hole-making equipment will account for a large part of your basic kit.

Electric drills are very convenient, providing you are near a source of power. If you have to make a repair afloat, or away from a power line, you need hand-operated tools. A simple wheel brace (left foreground of Fig. 1-2) will take drills up to about ¼ in. The effort needed to get a large drill through steel may be considerable, but in some circumstances it may be the only method available. For screw holes in wood or plastic, this is a convenient and easy tool to use, and it will insure that you won't accidentally go too deep. Your first small drill might be a wheel brace with twist drills in $^1/_{16}$-inch graduations up to ¼ inch. If you have an electric drill already, keep it handy anyway; it could be useful.

For larger holes in wood, the hand tool is a carpenter's brace with a moderate sweep. Bits with screw points will pull themselves into the wood with less effort on your part. A ratchet action is useful for working in situations where the brace cannot be turned completely. There are wood bits that can be used in an electric hand drill, but a brace with bits is more appropriate to a basic repair kit.

**Saws**

Like screwdrivers, the large range of saws available may not become obvious until you examine a catalog. The basic woodworking saw has teeth intended for cutting across the grain. This will cut along the grain also, but a saw with "rip" teeth for cutting along the grain cannot be used across the grain. A hand saw with crosscut teeth about 18 in. long is the most useful as the first saw. It is worthwhile paying enough to get good steel; a saw that quickly blunts is not worth keeping.

There are sets of saw blades which bolt into a common handle. These may be of value if you appreciate what each blade is intended for, but most of these sets do not include a blade which can take the place of the general-purpose crosscut saw. Some of these saws are claimed to be suitable for wood, metal, and plastics; but the characteristics of these materials really call for different tooth forms. The blades, therefore, are a compromise and are not very good for any of the materials.

Although woodworking saws may be sharpened—preferably by a specialist—metalworking saws have disposable blades. A 10 in. hacksaw frame is large enough for most repairs. Some have a compartment in the frame to carry spare blades. The frame should allow the blade to be turned and used parallel to an edge. Hacksaw blades do not last long, even in expert hands, so keep several spares.

There is much shaped work in boat repairs. Ashore, a workshop can cope with repairs with jigs and bandsaws; but if curves have to be cut afloat, the most useful hand tool is a coping saw with plenty of spare blades. With patience, curves can be cut in wood which is quite thick.

There is a "junior" hacksaw with a narrow blade about 5 in. long. Although not intended for curves, it is useful for cutting off small bolt ends or doing metal work too fine or awkward for a full-size hacksaw. A pad handle is also worth having; it can hold a short piece of hacksaw blade, a narrow woodworking "keyhole," or a hand saber saw (Fig. 1-7).

## Chisels, Knives, and Planes

Cutting tools are necessary for finishing wood to size and achieving a smooth surface. If much work is to be done on wood, a large range of chisels will eventually be needed. Start your collection with a ¾ in. chisel, preferably with beveled edges. This does all that a square-edge one does, and will get into corners. Later, you can add ¼ in., ½ in., and 1 in. chisels. Plastic handles will be secure on new chisels, but if you buy one secondhand, make sure there is a useful amount of blade left and the tang is secure in the handle.

Fig. 1-7. From left to right: two long, thin paring chisels (the narrow one being bevel-edged); a pad handle holding a keyhole saw; a backsaw over a partly cut piece of wood on a bench hook; a hole saw in the far background.

A plane is really a means of controlling the depth of a chisel cut. For general purposes, the blade should have a cap iron, which breaks off the shavings and reduces the risk of tearing up the surface of the wood. For repair work, a steel smoothing plane will tackle most jobs. The Stanley No. 4 or a comparable plane of other make is suitable.

A small block plane is also useful. This is about 5 in. long and can be held in one hand. Its blade, without a cap iron, is set at a low angle and is intended for work across the grain. This plane is used to follow a cut with a saw or to bevel an end. Knives with disposable thin blades are useful to have aboard. These sharp tools will cut rubber and soft plastic, mark out wood, and trim fiberglass that has partly cured. It is the sort of tool for which you find increasing uses.

A seaman's knife should also be in the basic kit. This may be a thin-bladed sheath knife or a clasp knife. A straightforward, good-quality plain knife is more satisfactory than one with many additional features. However, there should be a spike. This has its uses in splicing, marking hole positions on wood, or for pushing through holes in parts to bring them into line. This may be a proper marlinespike, but an icepick is just as good. For splicing, particularly the thicker fiber ropes,

22

a hardwood fir (spike) is kinder than a metal spike. One can be made by tapering an end on any piece of close-grained hardwood. It need not even be truly round.

Edged tools have to be sharpened occasionally. Sometimes they will have to be ground, but for quite long periods between grinding, they can be kept sharp with an oilstone. There are stones about 8 in. long with fine and coarse sides that will serve. The coarse side rubs away nicks caused by the nails, while the fine side restores the cutting edge. At one time. craftsmen used a variety of uncommon oils, but the practice today is to use a thin lubricating oil, or even kerosene. Always use oil; otherwise, the stone will wear unevenly and become clogged.

## Measuring Tools

In much repair work the measuring only consists of putting a piece in position like a template and marking directly on the job, without recourse to feet and inches or metric measure. Most boat parts are not at right angles, so there is not much use for a square. Anyone coming into boat repairing from jobs about the home where edges are straight and corners are square may have to adapt techniques to the new circumstances. However, there obviously have to be some measurements.

An expanding rule 6 or 10 ft long will take care of most measuring. It can be marked in feet and inches down to one-sixteenths, but with equipment getting more international, there may be some advantage in having one edge marked in metric measure. Another useful measuring tool is a 24 in. steel rule without a joint. Besides measuring, it is the basic straightedge and can be bent to mark moderate curves.

There should be a means of marking right angles. A combination square is a good buy. This has a sliding head on a rule (usually 12 in.) and can also be used to mark 45° angles (not often needed on a boat). With a pencil held against the end it can also be set to mark a line parallel to an edge, whether curved or straight (Fig. 1-8).

In repair work, it is most important to know what what you need, what its size should be, and anything else about it. This is particularly important if the boat is afloat or in some way far from your base or workshop. A notebook or a clipboard and plenty of paper should be an important part of your equipment. You need to adopt a systematic approach to the work and

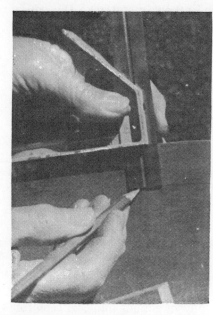

Fig. 1-8. Using combination square and a pencil as a gage to mark a line parallel to a curved edge.

become used to noting everything that has to be done. This also involves having a good supply of pencils as well as pens. Pencils are the wiser choice for marking wood, the marks being easier to remove or disguise later.

### Files

Files are to metal what planes and chisels are to wood. If you are to make or fit much metalwork, you will need to accumulate quite a big variety of them. They are graded by length and coarseness of cut. Some are provided with handles, but it is more usual for there to be a tang on the end of the file that fits into a handle bought separately. For a first file, the most generally useful is a 10 in. half-round type that gives a moderate cut. This has a flat and a curved side, but despite its name, it is not a true half-circle. A fine cut is better for finishing metal; but the first file, moderately coarse, will also work on wood without clogging.

### Painting Tools

Nearly all repair work involves painting or varnishing after the repair has been completed. Consequently, painting tools are basic to most jobs. Unfortunately, with the sporadic needs involved, paint brushes do not always get the treatment they need. If you are prepared to do all that is necessary to clean and preserve a brush after use, the best you can afford is the best investment. If you can't trust yourself to provide this care, there may be a good case for inferior brushes which can be discarded occasionally; also, care of brushes calls for various solvents and thinners which may not always be on hand during repair jobs.

Brushes are also needed for fiberglass work. If they are to last, they have to be cleaned with the appropriate solvent before resin has a chance to set in the bristles. This means that cleaning has to be carried on during the application of resin and fiberglass. If the resin sets only once in the bristles, no amount of solvent will soften it and the brush will have a hard patch (if it does not become completely hard) and be useless. Even the best fiberglass worker will spoil a brush occasionally, so the cheapest disposable brushes are best suited to this work.

Some manufacturers describe their best brushes as "varnish brushes." This does not mean they are unsuitable for paint—a brush for varnish is also good for paint, but for some painting you can make do with lesser quality. Where a large area is involved, particularly with modern finishes which dry quickly, a fairly broad brush is advisable; Widths of 3 or 4 in. should be selected. For more intricate work, there are brushes in widths from ¾ to 2 in. A narrow brush is needed for awkward angles, but the 1½ in. width is a good average choice. Several other tools are needed for preparing surfaces for painting, but these are detailed where the jobs are described.

## SCREWED FASTENERS

Screws are usually the most convenient form of fastening, and they come in a great variety of lengths, thicknesses, head types, and materials. Common steel woodscrews are unsuitable for work on boats because of rust. There are various protective platings on steel screws, but these generally only delay rather than prevent rusting. Common brass screws are often used, but brass is an alloy of copper and zinc. In salt water there is a risk that the zinc will gradually leave the alloy, the screw crumbling away in time. Unfortunately, all of the saltwater-resistant metals and alloys are considerably more expensive than common steel and brass screws. Brass screws are sometimes acceptable when their

| LENGTH | GAGE | LENGTH | GAGE |
|--------|------|--------|------|
| 1/2 | 4 | 1 1/4 | 10 |
| 3/4 | 4 | 1 1/2 | 8 |
| 3/4 | 5 | 1 1/2 | 10 |
| 3/4 | 6 | 1 1/2 | 12 |
| 1 | 6 | 2 | 10 |
| 1 | 8 | 2 | 12 |
| 1 1/4 | 8 | 2 1/2 | 12 |

Fig. 1-9. Common woodscrew and self-tapping screw sizes.

purpose is to pull parts together when glued; the glue eventually takes the strain, and failure of a screw later would not be serious.

Silicon-bronze and Monel metals are alloys that are seawater-resistant. They cost up to 1½ times as much as brass. Stainless steel screws are even better, but likely to cost twice as much as those made of brass.

Screw thickness is denoted by a gage number (higher numbers are thicker). Although the range of combinations of gages and lengths manufactured is large, only a few are commonly available. Suggested sizes for most purposes are shown in Fig. 1-9.

The common screw head is flat so that it presents a flush surface when countersunk (Fig. 1-10A). All sizes are also obtainable with round heads (Fig. 1-10B). Less common is an oval or raised head (Fig. 1-10C). This is particularly useful for holding panels which may have to be removed occasionally, and the head looks neat in a finishing or cup washer (Fig. 1-10D). Less common with wood screws, but sometimes seen in other screwed fastenings is the pan or cheese head (Fig. 1-10E). The fillister head (Fig. 1-10F) is a variation of this. Very large woodscrews may have square heads to accommodate a wrench. Sometimes the head will take both a screwdriver and a wrench.

Until a few years ago all screws had slotted heads to suit ordinary screwdrivers (Fig. 1-10G). Many still do, but for power driving in quantity production, a more slip-proof type became necessary. Several types of socket-head screws have been developed, but the most common is the Phillips head (Fig. 1-10H). For the usual range of screws in boats, no more

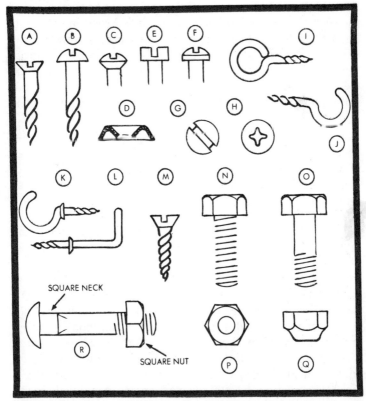

Fig. 1-10. The variety of configurations in screwed fasteners.

than three socket sizes are required, each with its own special screwdriver.

There are nylon-reinforced woodscrews; obviously, there is no corrosion problem and strength seems adequate, but care is needed to drill holes of the correct diameter and length if shearing is to be avoided.

A screw eye has a woodscrew end and a fully closed loop (Fig. 1-10I). A screw hook has an open eye (Fig. 1-10J). A cup hook as a shoulder and may be curved (Fig. 1-10K) or straight (Fig. 1-10L).

Self-tapping screws have their uses for making attachments to metal and plastic when a woodscrew cannot be used and the opposite side cannot be reached to use a nut on a machine screw. However, the common self-tapping screws used widely in the automobile industry are not suitable for boat conditions because they rust. Steel has to be used because the screw has to be hard enough to cut a thread in materials harder than wood. Stainless steel self-tapping screws are the only ones that should be used afloat. Their heads are similar to those of woodscrews (although countersink angles may be steeper) and sizes available are generally similar; but self-tapping screws are identified by the number of threads going right to the head (Fig. 1-10M).

For nut and bolt fastenings, it is advisable to get the nut, washer, and bolt (or screw) as a package. There are a number of thread types in use. Often imported fasteners are not compatible with domestic types and there is always the risk that odd nuts may not fit male threads, even if both are apparently the same size.

Screws are usually described in terms of their length and diameter in fractions of an inch, although some are given gage numbers and others are in a metric measurement. When the thread goes right to the head, it is a machine screw (Fig. 1-10N). When it only goes part way it is a bolt (Fig. 1-10O). Common nuts are hexagonal (Fig. 1-10P). Locknuts are thinner and are intended to be used with a common nut, using two wrenches to jam them against each other. However, it is much more usual now to use self-locking nuts, which make a friction fit at the top (Fig. 1-10Q). Another alternative is a locking compound (usually two-part epoxy) which adheres to the threaded parts but allows them to be forced apart with a wrench. Ordinary washers of the spring-steel type used under nuts on a boat would suffer from rust; there are stainless steel versions, but the other methods of locking are usually more convenient.

Machine screws may have any of the heads described for wood screws, although round and flat heads are most common. They may also have hexagonal heads for a wrench. Sometimes there are square heads and nuts, indicating tougher types. For wood there are carriage or coach bolts with a square neck under a snap head (Fig. 1-10R). This pulls into the wood and prevents the bolt from turning while the nut is tightenend.

## OTHER FASTENERS

Ordinary nails, as used for household carpentry, have no place on a boat. Galvanized, or otherwise coated with a seawater-resistant metal, they may have limited uses for rough work, but in general they should be avoided.

Some of the alloys used for boating screws will not stand up to hammer blows. Common brass is found in fine pins for light, plywood construction, but it is not usually found in larger nails. In any case, brass in contact with saltwater loses its zinc and deteriorates.

Much wood boatbuilding used to be done with copper nails and conical washers. Copper is a satisfactory metal for boat nails, but it is soft and holes have to be drilled to avoid bending them. Bronze nails can be driven into wood without having to drill holes first.

Ordinary iron nails are sometimes defined in "penny" sizes—a 2-penny nail is 1 in. long; a 20-penny nail, 4 in., and a 60-penny nail, 6 in. These definitions are best avoided when dealing with boat nails, but it might be a good idea to know the system in case a supplier describes his stock this way. Boat nails are normally described by length in inches, and fractions, and by a gage number—which differs from the gage used for screws. Larger sizes have lower numbers. As a rough guide, gage 8 is about ⅛ in. and gage 16, about $1/16$ in. Odd gage numbers are used, but even numbers are more common.

Nails normally have flat heads, but some boat nails have countersunk heads (Fig. 1-11A). Less common but sometimes found in large sizes, are diamond head nails (Fig. 1-11B). Copper boat nails may be square or round. If square, the gage size is the measurement across the flats. Ring-barbed nails are bronze and have rings cut in most of their length. The rings have a sawtooth cross section that resists being pulled out (Fig. 1-11C). Some of these nails tend to break if the shaft is too thin for their gage size. The shortest (up to 1 in.) should be gage 14. From 1 to 2 in., the gage should not be less than 12.

Many metal repairs will be made with machine screws, but if rivets are used, the metal of the rivets should match the metal being riveted. Exactly matching similar metals or alloys may not always be possible, as those rolled into sheets may not have the ductile qualities needed for rivets. Copper, iron, and aluminum rivets are available, although the latter are often unsuitable for saltwater conditions.

Rivets generally either have round snap heads (Fig. 1-11D) or countersunk heads (Fig. 1-11E). They are usually described by their length and diameter, in fractions of an inch, although very small ones may have gage sizes. In the aircraft industry, a considerable amount of riveting has to be done

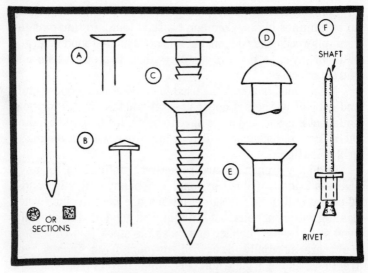

Fig. 1-11. Nails and rivets.

from one side only. Tools devised for this purpose have uses in boat repairing, as when fastening something to a hollow aluminum mast. The process is sometimes called *pop riveting*. Hollow rivets are used, each supplied on an iron, nail-like shaft (Fig. 1-11F). There are various lengths of aluminum alloy rivets, and common diameters are $3/32$ in., $1/8$ in., $5/32$ in., and $3/16$ in. When the rivet is inserted in a hole, the pointed end of the shaft is gripped in a tool which presses down on the rivet head and pulls the shaft so its head spreads the rivet on the other side. The shaft can be either broken off or pulled right through. Of course, tubular rivets are not watertight unless they are plugged, but for above-deck work, they have many uses.

Fasteners designed for attaching plastic-surfaced sheets or wallboards in homes can be used in boats, particularly inside cabins; but only water-resistant types should be chosen. Also useful are fasteners with plastic sleeves that expand by tightening a screw, without any need for access to the far side.

## TOOL STORAGE

A large investment in tools is necessary to deal with a comprehensive range of repairs. "Investment" is the right word, because the tools can save or earn a considerable amount of money—providing they are cared for. They all have to be protected against loss and damage; sharpened tools have to be protected against blunting, and steel tools have to be protected against rust.

If the workshop is normally heated, there will not be much rusting, particularly if the tools are frequently used. But when tools have to be taken to the boat special protection is needed. Plastic boxes with lift-out trays that are popular with fishermen are also very suitable for small tools, fittings, fasteners, and the many bits and pieces that soon accumulate in a boat repairer's kit.

Various types of wooden boxes are usually made for larger tools. It is best for the owner to make his own by first assembling the tools he wants to carry and devising a box to fit them. The hand saw will most likely govern the length of the box. As tools needed differ according to the work planned, too many internal fittings should be avoided. A box that can be carried on edge by its handle is convenient for most needs (see Fig. 1-3).

Unprotected wood may absorb water and affect the steel tools in the box. A wooden tool box should be assembled with waterproof blue and given as good a surface treatment as a wooden boat. A light color inside will encourage tidiness, and a bright color on the outside will make the box easily seen.

Protect saw teeth from possible damage caused by contact with other steel tools. Wood chisels and similar things may be placed in grooved pieces of wood (Fig. 1-12A) or they may be kept in a canvas roll (Fig. 1-12B). Planes may rest on wood pads, grooved to clear the blades (Fig. 1-12C). Metalworking files will soon lose their cutting ability if kept loose with other tools. They are best stored like wood chisels. Drill bits will suffer similarly. A wallet or container that has a slot for each drill is worth having.

Tools kept afloat for occasional use should be oiled or greased. However, grease can be a nuisance. A nonferrous tool may be preferable in the emergency kit, but for most cutting tools, there is no alternative to steel. Packing paper is available that will absorb water that would otherwise settle on the steel and cause rust. An alternative is to include a desiccant, such as some silica gel crystals in an open-weave bag to absorb moisture. The paper or the crystals can be dried out and used again.

If work is being done at sea, the probability of tools falling overboard has to be considered. For some jobs the risk has to

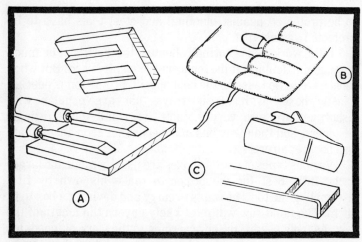

Fig. 1-12. Methods of storing tools to prevent blunted edges.

be taken, but as a precaution, use an apron with a pocket. Sailmakers traditionally used a short apron with a large pocket and a piece of cloth into which needles were stuck. The rigger has his knife, spike, and probably a pair of pliers, not only in a sheath on his belt, but also secured individually to ropes around his neck. Obviously, a tool dropped from aloft could be lethal to anyone below, yet too many lanyards would become impractical. If tools are carried in the pockets of clothes, try closing the pockets with Velcro; one hand will release it, yet its mere contact will secure it.

# Techniques and Improvisations

**2**

While standard tools and the techniques of using them have their place in boatbuilding and boat repair, the peculiarities of boats—particularly their shapes—call for methods different from those used by most other craftsmen. Parts have to be forced into shape and held there; shapes have to be marked when there are no straight lines or other data to work from. Things have to fit together when neither has a common base with the other. Parts may have to line up even when there is a solid, awkwardly curved hull between them. Traditional boatbuilders devised ways of overcoming these problems, many of which can be adapted to modern materials. The boat repairer should know about them.

C-clamps and other holding devices should as a matter of course be accumulated in a big range of sizes and patterns; but many occasions will arise when some alternative means of applying pressure will have to be devised. Wedges can often be used for this. The exact angle may not matter, but a wedge with a shallow slope will exert more pressure than one with a steep slope; as it is driven, it will only move the part being held a short distance, allowing a finer angular adjustment than can be afforded by a steeper-angled wedge.

A single wedge does not apply direct pressure; in some circumstances it will move the work sideways as it is driven. This may not matter, but a better way of applying direct pressure is to use *folding wedges*. These are a pair of wedges with identical angles, used under a pad or post and driven alternately from opposite sides.

Of course, the post may be a considerable length if necessary. It can reach from the wall or roof of the workshop to exert pressure on a plank being bent to shape. It can be used inside

Fig. 2-1. Wedges under the beams holding the boat allow fine adjustment for leveling and getting even support.

the boat against an engine support or other firm point to push out a deformed hull. The pressure exerted can be considerable. To avoid local damage use a strong board to spread the pressure (Fig. 2-2B). It is sometimes just as easy to get the pressure by a slightly overlong post driven sideways (Fig. 2-2C)—still a wedge action, but in a different form. Folding wedges can be used directly on the job, as when forcing in hull or deck planks tightly edgewise. The wedges are used against blocks of wood screwed temporarily to a frame or other structure (Fig. 2-3A). For a similar application where boards have to be glued to make up a width, a strip of wood can provide the basic pressure positions (Fig. 2-3B).

Parts to be clamped are usually not very massive. If thin pieces have to be held at many points, wedge cuts in scrap wood may be all that are needed (Fig. 2-3C). Sometimes pressure has to be applied some distance from an edge.

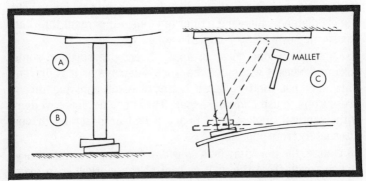

Fig. 2-2. Wedges used to exert pressure.

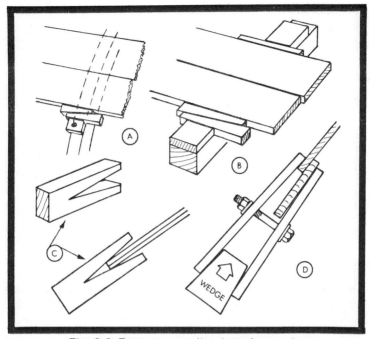

Fig. 2-3. Pressure applications for wedges.

C-clamps, limited by their shape, may not reach these places; but pressure can be applied by yet another application of the wedge. Two boards are loosely bolted together, the pressure end being enough from the bolt to reach the job. The other end is the same or a greater length; the longer it is, the more pressure can be applied by a wedge driven between the boards (Fig. 2-3D).

Repairs often have to be done away from workshop facilities and without a proper bench. The work may be held with a clamp, or a portable vise may be fixed to anything convenient, but there are improvised devices based on wedge action that can be used. A common problem is holding a thin piece of wood on edge for planing or other work. A piece of wood may be given a tapered notch and screwed to a board (Fig. 2-4A). This may be sufficient in itself, or a firmer grip can be obtained by using a wedge (Fig. 2-4B). For a long piece of work, two or more of these devices can be used.

A piece of wood too narrow to stand unaided on a temporary bench top can be pushed into a screwed down V-slotted block. If you have a strong board which you take to

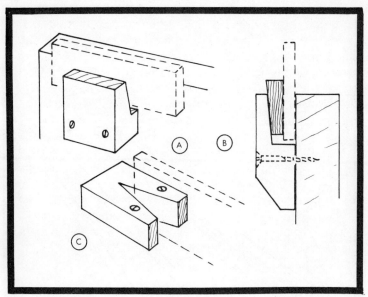

Fig. 2-4. How wedges can be used as substitutes for clamps.

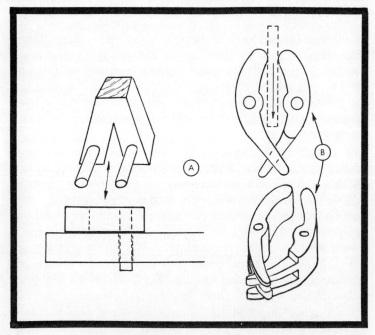

Fig. 2-5. Wedges as holding devices.

the job to act as a temporary bench, the *V*-block can be given a pair of dowels that drop into holes when required (Fig. 2-5A). For most purposes, a block of hardwood, 1½ in. thick and about 6 in. long, is suitable. There is a refinement of this, the construction of which will test your skill as a craftsman: Two interlocking pieces, each pivoting on a dowel, form a *V*; then, as the wood to be worked presses into the *V*, it is gripped on the sides by the noninterlocking ends (Fig.2-5B).

When the job has to be prevented from sliding while being worked on the flat side, a small strip of wood is usually nailed across the bench to hold it (Fig. 2-6); screws countersunk below the surface are safer than nails; however. The wood will make a better bench stop if it takes the pressure on the end grain  and is slightly beveled where it faces the work; otherwise, the top grain will soon break away and the edge will become rounded, making the stop much less effective.

## MARKING DEVICES

For marking out work on a boat, much use can be made of notched pieces of wood cut to resemble a square. For instance, a line can be drawn parallel to an edge, whether straight or curved, by holding a pencil against a piece of wood notched at the right distance (Fig. 2-7A). Suppose a plywood deck has to be fixed down before its edge is trimmed (the usual way in repairing a small boat). A piece of wood can have a slot cut in it to clear the plywood, the sides of which should be long enough to gage the distance in for the fasteners to follow parallel to the edge that will eventually be cut (Fig. 2-7B). A similar idea can be used to mark the line for a cut (Fig. 2-7C), but this may not be sufficiently accurate where the angle of the hull varies from a near right-angle to the deck, to considerable

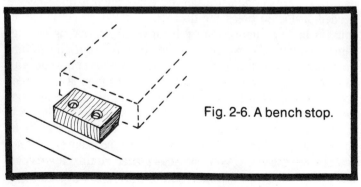

Fig. 2-6. A bench stop.

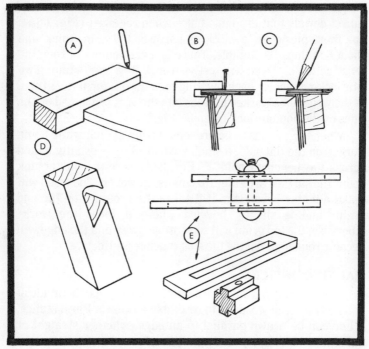

Fig. 2-7. Improvised marking gages.

flare. For this purpose, the gage is better made wide to maintain the side angle (Fig. 2-7D). For most repair work it is usual to notch scrap wood to make gages as needed, but a keen woodworker may make adjustable gages to suit many applications (Fig. 2-7E).

For marking lines square to an edge, the usual tool is a *try square*—when the edge is straight; but it is useless when a line has to be drawn against a curved edge. Such a line may be needed to locate holes for deck fittings. Some combination squares have a sliding central head which can be used (Fig. 2-8A); but with the exception of this tool, it is difficult to find anything really suitable. One can be made from plywood, say 15 inches long. The vital part of the construction is a straight edge which is at a right angle to, and bisecting, a line between two projecting pegs (Fig. 2-8B). The rest of the outline is a matter of choice. If the pegs, made from doweling, are glued in so as to project from each side, the tool can be used with either end against the work. With the pegs placed against a curve, a line drawn along the straight edge will be square to the edge

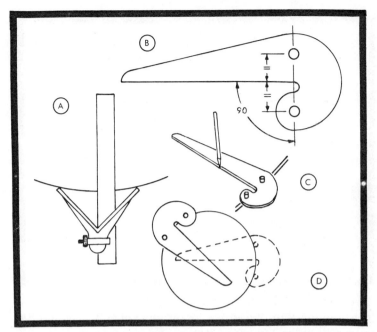

Fig. 2-8. Combination square and "round" square.

(Fig. 2-8C). A further use of the tool, which gives it its usual names of *center square* or *round square*, is in finding the center of a circle. Try it on a paint can; with the pegs against the rim, draw a line along the straight edge. Move to another position and draw another line. The point where the lines cross is the center (Fig. 2-8D). If you doubt it, try a third position. If you have made the tool accurately, any number of lines you make will cross in the same place.

## SPILING

A frequent problem in boat repairing is obtaining the shape of a part from the space it will have to occupy. Often it is in a position where there are few straight lines to work from, the job has a twist, or the position is nearly inaccessible. The boatbuilder uses variations on a method called *spiling*. The technique has to be adapted to individual circumstances, but a few examples of spiling will show how it is done.

In a simple case, a piece of wood is needed to make a locker top and the outer edge has to match the curve of the hull. It could be cut to the exact width and put in position as close to the hull as possible. But if a block of wood that is equal

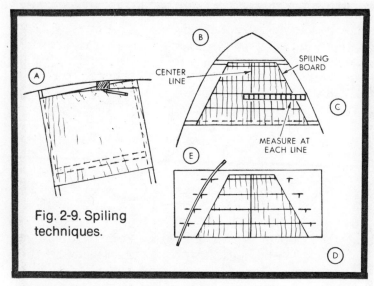

Fig. 2-9. Spiling
techniques.

in thickness to the greatest width of the gap is used with a
pencil to mark the curve, the locker top will only need a little
planing to make it fit (Fig. 2-9A).

In most cases, the actual piece cannot be marked while in
position. Suppose the locker top has to fit into the bow. The
position of the supporting members will give the outline, but
this has to be transferred to a piece of plywood that cannot be
tried in place until it is cut. Spiling can be done with a scrap
piece of plywood. Its straight edge is matched to the front edge
of the locker top and marked with lines parallel with this edge
that cross a perpendicular center line. (Fig. 2-9B). Accuracy
of the final curves will depend on the closeness of the parallel
lines, but 1 or 2 in. of separation should be satisfactory for
most jobs. Clamp the spiling piece in place and measure along
the parallel lines from the center line to the hull. Write this
measurement at each position (Fig. 2-9C). Remove the spiling
piece and put it on the plywood for the locker top. Make marks
at the appropriate distances extending along the lines (Fig.
2-9D). Bend a strip of wood through the points to mark the
curves (Fig. 2-9E).

Reading and noting measurements can lead to mistakes,
particularly when working in awkward places. Another
method of spiling, done without measuring, is often preferable.

Suppose a bulkhead is needed for a stern locker which is to
be a short distance forward of the transom (crossbeam) in an

open boat. A board is clamped across the upper edges of the boat's sides at the right position and a piece of plywood is temporarily hung from it. Its size and shape is not important, but it should not be more than about 9 in. from the hull at any point; a little experience will show what spacing is acceptable for a particular job (Fig. 2-10A). A center line would be useful. Prepare a *spiling stick*: a flat, straight piece of wood, square at one end and cut diagonally at the other to form a point (Fig. 2-10B). Somewhere between 1 and 2 ft would be a suitable length.

Place the spiling stick against the spiling board (plywood) at a number of places, putting the point against the skin and marking around the opposite end and the long side that lead to the point. In particular, do this at chines[1], stringers[2], and anything else that has to be cut around. Where there is a curve, use the spiling stick at enough points to get the effect of the curve, closing the spacing on tight curves (Fig. 2-10C). Although a hull should be symmetrical, many are not; to

[1]The intersections of the bottom and sides of a boat.

[2]A longitudinal reinforcing timber.

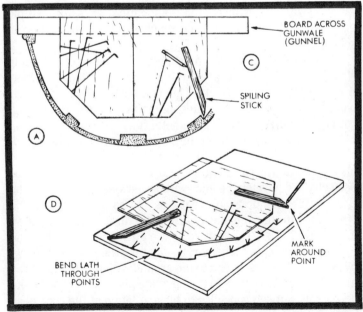

Fig. 2-10. Transferring dimensions without a direct measurement.

insure symmetry, spile both sides. The alternative is to make half a template from the spiling on one side and use it to check the opposite side before cutting the bulkhead panel.

After marking all the points on the spiling board, put it in position on the wood to be used for the bulkhead. Reposition the spiling stick in each place and mark around its point (Fig. 2-10D). This gives you points for the final outline, which can be joined by straight lines where appropriate, or by bending a strip of wood through the points to get a curve.

## LAYING

There are occasions when the boat repairer is faced with the need to lay out something fairly large, either on the floor or on one or more sheets of plywood held together. If a new frame has to be made, either from spiling in the boat or from an original drawing, an absolutely straight base line of maybe 10 ft will have to be crossed by another line precisely at a right angle to it and almost as long—if the two halves of the frame are to be symmetrical and the whole width is to be accurate. Errors in straightness or angle could upset the final result.

This sort of thing is easy enough to deal with on a drawing board, or on the job within the confines of a 2 ft rule; but in larger sizes, it involves the application of some simple geometry, although on a scale much larger than learned in school.

A stretched cord is the most accurate means of obtaining straightness. To draw a straight line of any length on the floor, it is best to use a *chalk line*. This is a strong cord, as thin as possible and preferably made of hairy natural fiber (e.g. cotton) rather than smooth synthetic fiber. If you are working alone, tie a loop in the end of the cord and fix it to the floor with an awl (Fig 2-11A). Walk back from the awl, letting the cord play out while you rub it with ordinary chalk. When enough has been chalked, stretch the line (without jerking it), hold it to the floor with one thumb and reach as far as possible with the other hand to snap the line by lifting it a few inches and letting it go (Fig. 2-11B). This will deposit a straight line of chalk on the floor. If you have a helper, he can take the place of the awl by holding the starting end to the ground with his thumb. If the line needed is more than 20 ft long, instead of reaching to strike it yourself, get someone else to lift and let go of the cord near its middle. If you are working on a light surface, try using charcoal instead of chalk.

The corner of a sheet of plywood can usually be trusted to form a right angle. It can be used as a *set square* for drawing a right angle (within the limits of its size). It is never advisable to, say, mark a right angle with 6 ft sides by guessing at an extension from a right-angle object with 4 ft sides. It is always better to use a means of drawing a right angle with sides longer than you actually need. Any risk of error will be reduced; the extending method may increase an error.

The most favored way of marking a right angle is generally known as the 3:4:5 *method*. This is based on the fact that if a triangle is drawn with the sides in the proportion of 3, 4, and 5, the angle between the two shorter sides will be a right angle. The units used can be anything convenient to suit the size of the job. If the long side of the right angle has to be 8 ft long, the short side will be 6 ft long—and the longest side of the triangle will be 10 ft long.

To derive a right angle using this method, first measure four units to form a base line and make a mark (Fig. 2-11C). From one end of the line (the right end in the drawing), strike a short arc using a cord 3 units long. If you have a tape measure with a looped end, stick an awl through it while you hold a pencil against the tape at the appropriate distance. Similarly, you could use a piece of wood with an awl pushed

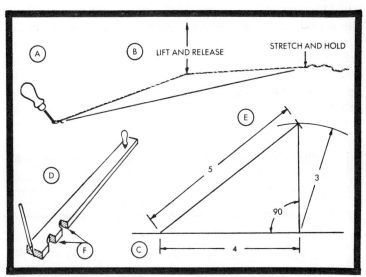

Fig. 2-11. Using an awl in combination with a cord or board to derive right angles.

through it at the right distance from one end. Holding a pencil against the end produces something like a compass (Fig. 2-11D). The arc need only be as long as you judge necessary to cross the region where the short side will intersect it. Strike an arc 5 units long from the other end of the line (the left end in the drawing) so that it intersects the first arc (Fig. 2-11E). When the intersection point of the two arcs is connected to the ends of the base line, a right triangle will be produced.

Your work may necessitate that other lines be drawn; they should all be measured from these first lines to maintain accuracy. The surest way to obtain accuracy in other lines is to draw arcs, then have an assistant help you to strike lines through them. If several distances are needed, one piece of wood can be used as a compass by marking the position of a number of notches for the pencil (Fig. 2-11F).

Another useful tool for laying out and other marking jobs is a pair of *trammel heads* (Fig. 2-12). They are not easy to obtain new, but may be found secondhand. The heads have sockets to fit a strip of wood, with screws to clamp them in any position. Usually each head has a projecting point; sometimes there is provision for clipping on a pencil in place of one point. The trammel heads, on a suitable strip of wood, can be used instead of the notched wood and awl.

One method is completely independent from the proportions of a right triangle. Again, a base line is drawn. Then the trammel heads or the wood-and-awl are adjusted to an arbitrary length that at least exceeds half the length of the base line. So adjusted, the marking tool (Fig. 2-13A) is used to strike two arcs, from each end of the base line, and extending above and below it (Fig. 2-13B). The intersection points of the arcs are then connected. The line that results will be perpendicular to the base line.

Another way of making a right angle with trammels, particularly if it has to be close to the end of the base line, uses the fact that if a triangle is drawn so that one side is the

Fig. 2-12. Trammel heads.

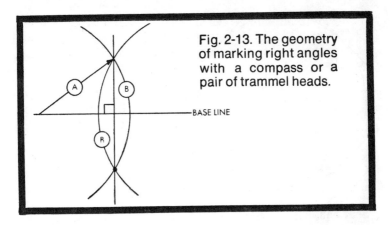

Fig. 2-13. The geometry of marking right angles with a compass or a pair of trammel heads.

BASE LINE

diameter of a circle, the angle at the apex touching the circumference is a right angle. This method requires that you make a mark on the base line a convenient distance from the point at which the right angle is needed (starting point in Fig. 2-14). A compass or a pair of trammel heads is then adjusted to this length and used to strike two arcs (Fig. 2-14A) that intersect. The compass pin is placed at the intersection point (B) and a circle is drawn—or at least enough of one to fall in the approximate region where you suspect the missing side will be. Next, a line (C) is drawn from the first mark on the base line through the center of the circle to its circumference. When that point on the circumference is connected by a line (D) back to the starting point, a right angle will result.

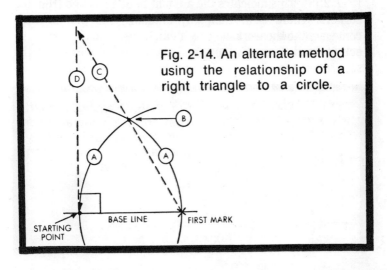

Fig. 2-14. An alternate method using the relationship of a right triangle to a circle.

STARTING POINT     BASE LINE     FIRST MARK

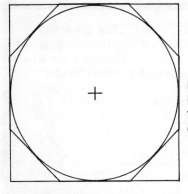

Fig. 2-15. Drafting instruments could be used to form an octagon from a circle drawn within a square.

## Spar Shaping

If a piece has to be spliced onto a broken spar, or a round replacement is needed, the wood will almost certainly have to be shaped from a square section. A short piece might be turned on a lathe, but the average lathe is incapable of working the larger pieces that are likely to be needed in most boat repairs. Making round what is a square by hand on a bench is not difficult if tackled systematically. The square is first reduced to a regular octagon, then its eight corners are removed to make sixteen sides, and so on. Providing the eight sides are carefully worked, the other shaping can be safely done by eye.

If a circle is drawn within the square section, drafting instruments can be used to draw lines touching the circle at 45° (Fig. 2-15). This indicates the amount to be removed from the corners. There is another way of doing this that is more convenient to the workshop, as it can be done on the end of the actual wood. Draw two diagonals between the corners of the square section (Fig. 2-16A), and strike an arc (Fig. 2-16B).

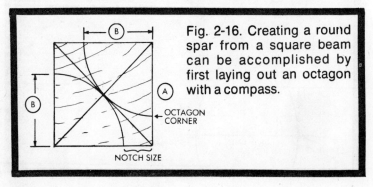

Fig. 2-16. Creating a round spar from a square beam can be accomplished by first laying out an octagon with a compass.

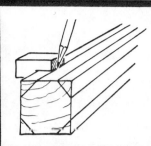

Fig. 2-17. A piece of wood is notched as a marking gage for preliminary spar shaping. The legs of the notched piece are as long as the distance from the stricken arc to the nearest corner of the square beam section.

This marks the corner of the octagon. This can be done from all corners, but marking once gives the measurement needed for gaging along the spar. Use a piece of wood with a notch cut to the size derived in Fig. 2-16 to mark the beam for the octagonal cuts (Fig. 2-17).

If you have a fully equipped workshop, it may be possible to take off the waste wood with a spindle-molder or other power tool, but under usual conditions the waste will have to be removed by planing. The longer the plane, the easier it will be to keep the sides true.

The job may be held in a vise if it is a short piece. If it is very long, you can prevent it from bending by working on the top of the bench or a stiff board. A trough can be made to hold this sort of work (Fig. 2-18A). A piece across one end acts as a stop to plane against. For a piece of spar longer than the trough, a small extension trough without the stop can be added. Another method of supporting the spar and preventing it from rolling is to employ a series of identical notched blocks (Fig. 2-18B).

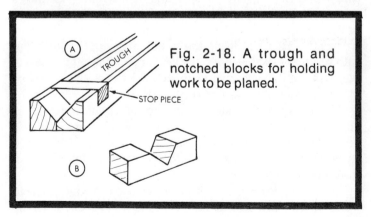

Fig. 2-18. A trough and notched blocks for holding work to be planed.

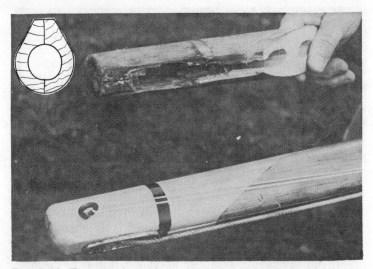

Fig. 2-19. The damaged top of a dinghy mast has been cut off and a new piece grafted on. This was built up in two pieces and hollowed (see inset) to match the remaining part.

When the spar has been planed to an octagon of reasonably symmetrical form, further work should be done in cross lighting. The shadowed areas defined by the octagon's facets will then allow you to plane off high spots and get a very nearly round form. A block plane held in one hand while you rotate the work with the other to find high spots is a convenient way of working in the last stages.

After the spar is planed as round as possible, use sandpaper, first around the spar and then with the grain. To remove plane marks it is convenient to sit on the spar on a braced framework while you sand the ends; turn the spar frequently. This will leave the wood satisfyingly round, but with scratches around it. Even if not very obvious at this stage, they will show up under varnish; so finish the work by sanding in the direction of the grain to remove the crosswise marks.

Spars are usually made of spruce or other soft wood. If it is unprotected, it will soon absorb dirt or become bruised. It is advisable to give the wood at least one coat of varnish as soon as possible, *even if it has to be rubbed off* at some later stage in the repair.

A spar made from a single piece of wood is always prone to warping. This can be counteracted if the wood is cut down the

48

middle and one piece is turned end for end; then the pieces are glued together for shaping. Of course, if the repair piece has to be spliced to an original hollow spar (Fig. 2-19) it will have to be cut through, grooved, and glued (photo inset).

If it is a mast that is being replaced or repaired, it will probably be tapered. This is treated in much the same way as a spar with parallel sides. The wood is planed to the taper while still square. The beveling to make an octagonal section will have to taper, but using a simple notched piece of wood will not give a correct limit to the bevel at all points. If the piece is not very long, the positions at each end can be marked, then a straightedge used to draw the lengthwise lines. For a long taper, a special notched gage has to be used (Fig. 2-20A). This is made to just fit over the wood at the thick end. The legs of the notch are tapered to thin edges. The position to be marked is nicked into the edge of the wood to take the point of a pencil. If drawn along the length of the tapered beam to keep the edges close to the wood all the time, the pencil will automatically follow the edge of a tapering octagon. As with the simple notched piece, the gage will have to be used eight times, working both ways from each corner of the section. An alternative is to use pegs and nails in a board as a gage (Fig. 2-20B). As the gage is pulled along with the pegs in contact with the tapering spar, the nails scratch the bevel lines.

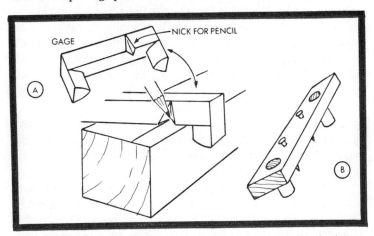

Fig. 2-20. A gage used to maintain an octagonal shape throughout the length of a tapered, square beam (A). An alternative is a board with pegs and nails (B); the application is almost identical.

# SANDING

Smoothing a surface with an abrasive paper is usually referred to as "sanding," but sand as the abrasive ceased to be used a long time ago. It was followed by powdered glass; this sort of abrasive paper is still favored by some woodworkers. Normally, it has particles of glass, held to backing paper with glue which is sensitive to dampness. If the paper is soaked in water, the glass will fall off. Even in damp conditions the grip of the glue will be lessened and the glass will rub away soon after the paper is used. This can be prevented by warming the paper before use until the glue feels stiff when flexed.

The traditional equivalent of glass-coated paper for metalwork has been emery paper. This is still available, although a cloth backing is more usual than paper.

Garnet was an early alternative to glass, and paper coated with this grit is still being used. Aluminum oxide is a more recent abrasive grit, while silicon carbide has nonclogging qualities that make it attractive.

The particles on a sheet of abrasive paper are fairly uniform in size. Unfortunately, there is no uniform system of grading applicable to all kinds of abrasive papers; but the more recent grits have numbers, the lower numbers corresponding to the coarser grades. Number 50 is about the coarsest grade likely to be needed in boat repair; No. 80 is a medium grade; No. 120 is for fine sanding; No. 180 or 220 are for getting the smoothest finishes. Some manufacturers indicate grades in a different way; along with their equivalent markings they are: No. 1 (50), No. 1/0 (80), No. 3/0 (120), and No. 6/0 (220). Yet another method that may be applied to glass grits denotes M2 as the medium grade (the M meaning middle). A finer grade is F2 (meaning *fine* 2). A coarser grade is S2 (meaning *strong* 2). A finer grade is 1½, while the finest is *flour* paper. A really coarse grade is S3. Fortunately, this cumbersome method of grading is almost obsolete, but these notes will help if you encounter the markings.

Abrasive paper is not cheap and it is unwise to use it in a wasteful manner. Sheets are usually 9 in. by 11 in. If a sheet is folded and used in the hand, it will soon wear out. It is much better, both in effect and for economy, to tear the sheet into four small squares and hold it over a block of wood or a proper sanding block of either cork or rubber-faced wood. For some work it may be possible to work with one-eighth of a sheet at a time. The sheet can be torn by placing it on a hard surface, grit side down, and pulling it against the edge of a steel rule.

Modern grits are bonded to the paper or cloth backing with waterproof glue. Some work best if kept wet. This reduces the tendency of the grit to become clogged and allows the paper to be used longer. The wetted paper also helps to achieve a smooth finish when rubbing down hard-setting paints and varnishes. This type of abrasive paper is sold as *waterproof* or *wet-and-dry*.

All of the foregoing notes apply to abrasive materials for hand use, but similar grits are used for power sanders. In general, the grit for power work is coarser than the grit used for the equivalent handwork. The power action seems to give a smoother result than when the same grit is used by hand.

The simplest sanding machine is a disk sander, a circle of abrasive paper fixed to a rubber backing and driven by an electric drill. It is not a finishing tool. It can be used to quickly abrade a surface that might be difficult to reduce by other means, but the surface will have curved scratches from the rotating action. A careful worker can keep the final effect inconspicuous, but usually further work with another tool is needed to bring the surface to a satisfactory finish.

A belt sander is a heavier and more expensive tool which uses a continuous belt of abrasive; it makes scratches in a straight line, but they can be arranged to conform to the direction of the grain. With a coarse-grit belt this sander can deal with unevenness like no other tool can; with a fine belt, it will produce a finished surface.

An orbital or vibrating sander is a light tool that is either self-powered or used an attachment to an electric drill: A flat piece of abrasive paper on a pad vibrates at a high speed over a small "orbit." It is not directional in the scratches it produces so can be used in any direction, but its effect is rather slow. It's most commonly used with fine abrasive paper to flatten a surface before painting, or between coats of paint. The effect is like hand sanding, but because of the high, uniform speed the result is more even.

There are other means of applying an abrasive. Oarmakers famous for their varnished racing oars use pumice powder on a cloth to rub down the varnish between coats on their graceful spruce blades. Steel wool is sometimes used on wood as an abrasive, but it can leave tiny particles of steel embedded in the grain. In the necessarily damp conditions on a boat, these could cause rust marks. If this method of preparing a wood surface is to be used—and most experts would rather not—*bronze wool* should be used.

A few sheets or partial sheets of different grades of waterproof paper in the repair kit will handle all the rubbing down likely to be needed for any type of material. Leave glass and garnet papers, and any other nonwaterproof types, in the workshop.

## PAINTING

The choice of *paint* for particular materials and special instructions for their use is covered in the chapter on those materials, but the tools and techniques common to all painting jobs can be described here.

Repairs may have to be painted or varnished in other than ideal conditions, but the best can be made of most circumstances. Surfaces should be dry and clean. If there is dirt on the surface, whatever the base material, the paint will just adhere to the dirt; the strength of the paint film will be no better than the strength of the layer of dirt. Some impurities may actually reject the paint. Paint cannot be expected to adhere to a film of water, however thin; so it is no use trying to put paint on any wet material.

Most paints are sensitive to cold. Something in the range of 50° to 80°F is considered optimum for painting. Very humid weather should be avoided as dampness may penetrate the wood and reduce adhesion. Try to avoid winds—they may blow dust onto the wet paint. If insects become ensnared in the wet paint and cannot get off, leave them until the paint is hard; then they can be removed without leaving much of a mark. Also, try to avoid letting the finish dry in direct sunlight.

The consistency of some paints can be critical. In general, a better result can be had when two thin coats are applied rather than one thick one. Thick coats may leave brush marks, or dry unevenly. Many varnishes do not require stirring, but most paint pigments settle in the bottom of the can. Leave the can upside-down for awhile before opening it. Although a mechanical stirrer has its uses, too rapid agitation will cause many bubbles which will have to be left to rise to the surface and disperse—and then the paint will need stirring again. A mechanical stirrer should definitely *never be used for varnish*.

Stirring with a piece of wood is all that is needed. If the stirred paint appears too thick, the thinners specified by the makers should be used sparingly. It is very easy to thin excessively; and nothing can be done to put this right, except adding more paint. The character of many antifouling paints is the reverse of that of varnish—they require stirring almost continuously during use.

The painting or varnishing of repairs will almost certainly have to be done by brushing. Good paint brushes are expensive; for the best work, however, they are absolutely essential. Cheap throwaway brushes are only acceptable if you are prepared to accept less than the best finish. If the existing paint is poor and you do not intend to finish with an all-over paint job, cheaper tools may not matter. Natural bristles are advisable for varnish. Nylon brushes are suitable for most paints, but the solvents in some paints will attack the bristles; look for any warning to this effect on the can.

If a brush is to be kept in proper condition from one job to the next, it will need careful maintenance. There may be little harm done by standing a brush in water if it is used for the same paint the next day, but it is not considered professional practice. It is better to suspend the brush in a mixture of two parts raw linseed oil to one part turpentine. Suspend the brush by putting a wire through a hole in the handle, so the metal *ferrule* is just above the surface of the liquid and the bristles do not touch the bottom of the container.

Before applying the paint, carefully wipe the brush on paper or scrap wood. Vigorous slapping is not necessary. If the brush is no longer required for a particular paint, it has to be cleaned, preferably with the thinner recommended on the paint can. Turpentine may be used with normal paints, but for some synthetics, the only solvent that will work is the one that goes with the particular paint.

No matter how much solvent is used, it is likely that some of the pigment will remain in the bristles. The next step is to work out the pigment with warm water and soap (or detergent), while manipulating the bristles and squeezing out the brush many times. Finally, wash it in clean water, squeeze it out, and leave it to dry. Wrap the end in paper and lay the brush flat in storage.

There are special preparations for cleaning brushes other than the recommended solvents that work with many paints.

There are others to remove hardened paint, but however a caked brush is treated, it will never be suitable for good work again—there is no complete cure.

Paint rollers are more applicable to household interior painting than to marine painting, although sometimes they are useful on decks. Common spray guns have their uses for some sorts of paint, but their use will hardly be justified for most repair painting; the paint has to be thinned, and a source of air pressure is needed. The latest technique is airless spraying, but the equipment is seldom available to the amateur. However, if a fairly large area has to be painted, possibly as the final overall finish after a repair has been touched up, a spray gun will produce a smoother and quicker job than brushing. Because sprayed paint cannot be kept within bounds by the operator, adjoining paintwork, glass, and anything else not intended for painting, should be masked.

Achieving a good result with a spray gun is largely a matter of practice. If you have any doubt about your ability, stick to brushing.

For the few square feet of an average repair, it may be satisfactory to use the paint directly from the can. But if there is much to do, use a proper paint bucket into which you can tip the amount of paint needed. This is even more important with varnish. Decanting paint or varnish from the original container can help you avoid skin contamination. Whether you work from the original can or another container, it is a good idea to fix a thin rod across the top, possibly through the holes provided for a handle. Instead of wiping the brush on the edge of the can, you wipe it on the wire.

Painting with a brush may seem like a simple enough job, but it is easy for a beginner to finish with runs or curtains—a surface very different from what an expert would achieve. For best results, dip not more than about two-thirds of the bristles in the paint and wipe the excess out on the wire. Use the brush in several directions on the job to work the paint as far out as it will reasonably go on the surface, but make the final strokes in the direction you would wish any brush marks to be; they may not disappear during drying. Normally, this would be in the long direction of the thing being painted, but if you have any choice, or the direction does not matter, finishing with an upward stroke will help prevent runs.

As you progress with the painting, arrange things so the final strokes of each stage go towards the previous stage. If you brush back over the edge of the previous stage and lift the brush at the same time, the paint film should dry without any signs of overlap. With some quick-drying paints you may have to work quickly so that the edges of painted areas don't dry before the new paint can be tapered out over them.

The same idea should be used to blend new paint onto the edges of existing paintwork around a repaired area. Take first coats only a little way over the sanded, tapered edge of the old paint. When rubbing down between coats, pay particular attention to these overlaps and blend the paint into about the same level as the original paint. The top coat should then finish at the same level as the earlier top coat. No matter how skilled you are, the position of new work will almost certainly be visible, although only very slightly. The only sure coverup is an overall painting.

Masking tape is the answer for well defined, joining areas of paint. If the repaired area covers two or more colors of paint, masking tape will allow cleaner lines. Paint the lighter color first; this way, if it overlaps its eventual limiting line, it won't matter. Cover the first coat with masking tape (when it's dry) along the line, and paint the next color. Use two strips if the color has to be confined to a band. If the paint is to be sprayed, masking tape alone will not be sufficient protection for surrounding paintwork. It should be covered with newspaper, wrapping paper, or similar material held in place with masking tape to outline the limit of the paint (Fig. 2-21). Some paints cure extremely hard; removing the masking tape may be difficult if it is left until the paint is dry. It is usually better to carefully peel off the masking tape when the paint has just lost its tackiness.

Varnish and some of the synthetic paints do not take kindly to conventional working out by spreading. If the paint instructions warn against this, or advise "flowing" on, be warned. Instead of working these coatings in several directions before brushing out towards the previous paint, use a moderate amount of varnish or paint on the brush and apply it with two or three strokes from the new surface towards the previous one. Try to spread the paint with a minimum of brushwork. The problem is to get just sufficient spread without

Fig. 2-21. In preparation for spraying the upper part of this hull, the lower part is protected by paper and the paint line defined with masking tape.

leaving an excess anywhere—particularly on a vertical or sloping surface where drips or runs could develop. Look at earlier coats as you progress, and lift drips with your brush as they appear.

Modern finishes dry quickly, so the period when runs occur are brief, but this also means that if they form undetected curtains, it may be too late to do anything about them. Warm varnish, thinly applied, covers a surface best, even if it means more coats. Varnish is much easier to apply on a warm, windless day. As ideal conditions may not always exist, you have to do what you can to simulate them. Standing varnish in hot water to raise its temperature will thin it and make it easier to apply smoothly. A hot day will naturally warm the varnish to a workable consistency. Painting instructions applicable to particular materials will be found in the chapters concerning them (fiberglass, wood, metal, and ferroconcrete).

There is no universally acceptable paint for all materials, but the paint on a repair should match that originally used if possible. A two-part epoxy paint is the best to carry in an emergency repair kit for temporary protection of almost any material. Choose one with the quickest setting time.

# Working With Fiberglass

**3**

Fiberglass is a word that became part of the boatbuilding lexicon early in the 1950s and went on to become the most important boat construction material. Fiberglass is not really a very correct description of the whole material. The trade references FRP, meaning *fiberglass reinforced plastic,* and GRP, meaning *glass reinforced plastic,* are more descriptive of its construction. A boat or any structure built with this material is really made of synthetic resin reinforced with spun glass filaments, of which a trade name is Fiberglas.

Anyone tackling a repair should know something about construction materials and be able to assess how the hull to be worked on was made. Fortunately, new materials can be made to bond satisfactorily to the old ones; a properly made repair should reinstate the hull to as good as new structurally, even if sometimes the finish is not as good as the original.

Fiberglass is formed from spun glass filaments, extremely fine individually, gathered together into groups or threads. Glass in this form has little in common physically with sheet glass. The threads are formed into reinforcing material in a great many ways. The glass threads may be woven into mats or cloths, sometimes the same way fabrics are made, but usually in a fairly coarse form; tapes in various widths are made the same way. Woven cloth material is expensive and not necessarily better for all purposes; so the cheaper forms, built up of short chopped strands, are more commonly used. *Chopped strand mat* has a random mixture of short pieces compressed together and held with a light binder which dissolves in resin. In another method, short strands are deposited during manufacture in a random fashion with liquid resin and an air gun. However, despite attempts at mechanization in manufacture, much boat construction is done by hand—the method which will have to be used in repair work.

Nearly all fiberglass-reinforced plastic boats are made of polyester resin. But although it is the usual choice for repair work, epoxy will bond with the original polyester and is usually preferred.

Although the chemicals needed are usually inter-changeable between brands, it is generally advisable to get them all from one source. Several firms supply fiberglass repair kits for small repairs. The resin is supplied as a liquid of syrupy consistency, usually nearly colorless. In this form it has quite a long pot life. To set it, quite small quantities of other chemicals have to be added. These are a *catalyst* and a promoter (also called accelerator). Once these are added, setting commences and nothing will reverse the process. There are other additives for special purposes. Thixotropic resin is used to reduce the risk of running on vertical surfaces. Chalklike fillers are used to make the mix opaque, and to give the mixture more body. Color pigments may be added. Although this is a good idea for new construction, it is very difficult to match colors in a repair, and it is more usual to paint the old and new work to get an even appearance.

Almost as important as the correct chemicals in the right proportions is the working temperature. The suppliers of the materials will specify this, but a minimum around of 50°F is usually required. There are different polyester mixes for lower temperatures, but if the work is attempted at a very low temperature, the resin may either never set completely or take weeks to become safe to use. Follow the minimum temperature instructions included with the resin. Higher working temperature ·specifications indicate very quick setting times; sometimes the resin will gel so quickly that the work cannot be terminated within the setting period. Extremes of indicated working temperature may make emergency repairs difficult if nothing can be done about controlling the temperature in the work area.

Nearly all professionally built fiberglass craft are made with several close layers of spun glass embedded in resin in mat or cloth form. In smaller boats, the total thickness is no more than ⅛ in. or so; in large craft, it is seldom more than ⅜ in.—except in areas where a great load has to be taken. If you see a boat with material that seems excessively thick, it may be because the boat is of a sandwich construction—almost certainly a one-off, amateur effort. The sandwich may consist of balsa wood or a plastic foam between layers of reinforced resin. The sandwich material gives stiffness to comparatively flat panels and lends itself to building individual boats with simple molds. The normal method is more suitable for quantity production; the work expended can be justified if its cost can be spread over many boats.

## MINOR REPAIRS

The outer surface of a fiberglass boat is formed by a *gel coat*, a layer of resin that is pressed on with a highly polished mold; the surface of the mold is reproduced in the gel coat and accounts for the glossy appearance of a new boat. The gloss does not last indefinitely, however. The finish will have to be polished occasionally. Boat polishes are akin to car polishes; those containing carnauba wax give the most durable results.

However well the polishes work, hulls and decks will become damaged with scratches and dents that go through the gel coat. These are unavoidable in normal use and represent the most commonly needed minor repairs. If the damage is deep enough to expose the fiberglass threads, there is a risk of capillary attraction causing moisture to flow into the area around the damage. A small amount of absorption is not serious, and inevitable underwater; but it should be avoided by repair where possible—particularly if the boat is subjected to freezing temperatures. If moisture in the laminations freezes, it will expand and cause the hull to wrinkle or pucker.

Although hulls are made of polyester resin, there is a choice between using polyester or epoxy resin for repairs. In large quantities, epoxy is much more expensive; for more extensive repairs, polyester is the usual choice. But for minor damage there are advantages in epoxy. In the amount normally needed, the difference in cost is negligible.

Epoxy has a longer pot life than polyester and will remain usable longer in a shipboard repair kit. While newly mixed polyester will bond satisfactorily with old, hard polyester in a hull, epoxy makes a better bond in a situation where damage is slight and undercutting or beveling edges for extra grip is out of the question.

When a fiberglass boat is made from a mold, some of the release compound clings to the boat; in spite of hard use after a considerable time, traces of it will still remain. Even if the surface has never been waxed, it is important to clean around the part to be repaired to remove any remaining release compound. If wax or polish has been used, cleaning is doubly important. If a repair is attempted without cleaning, the new material will only be joined to a film of contaminants and have minimal strength.

Scratches and dents should be scraped out with a spike or knife blade to remove dirt and to roughen the surface. This is best followed by wiping with solvent. There are dewaxing preparations available, and some paint manufacturers have their own recommended polish and release compounds. But if time allows, wash the fiberglass with a stiff brush and warm detergent solution, followed with a fresh-water rinse. When the surface is dry, wipe it with a cloth soaked in mineral spirits. *Do not* use brush cleaners or paint thinners.

For a simple scratch or dent which has penetrated the gel coat, two-part epoxy resin is required. Squeeze out equal amounts (or per the maker's directions) onto a piece of wood or plastic, mix them thoroughly with a spatula or stick, and press the mixture into the ding. Make sure there are no air bubbles. Epoxy does not shrink noticeably as it sets, so except for leaving a very slight amount standing above the surface for sanding, there is no need to build up the repair. A piece of cellophane can be put over the resin while it cures. This is especially helpful in a place where the resin might run out of the crack. The same thing can be done with polyester. It tends to shrink as it sets, but for a small repair this can be ignored.

Epoxy used to take a considerable time to set, but this has been shortened. One manufacturer offers 1½ hours working time and 6 hours setting or curing time; another, ½ hour for working and 4 hours for curing. Some polyester mixtures set very fast, with a few minutes working time and 30 minutes curing. For a small repair this is attractive, but if there is much to be done, the mixture will become stiff and unspreadable before it is applied. When it reaches this stage, it has no use and must be scrapped. If more than can be mixed on a board is needed, a throwaway container should be used.

Curing takes place in two stages. The resin gels to a semihard state comparatively quickly, then takes considerably longer to become really hard. If the state is judged correctly after gelling, it is possible to trim the still fairly soft surplus with a sharp knife or razor blade to fairly near the surface level. Trying this too early will pull resin out of the scratch. Trying it too late will prove impossible. In any case, neither epoxy nor polyester lends itself to careful smoothing like putty. They are too sticky when first applied.

Trimming with a knife will not give a finished surface. If it happens that too much is cut away, or the curing resin shrinks below the surface, more resin can be mixed to bond with that below. In any case, when the repair has finally cured, it must be filed or sanded level with the surrounding surface. The surrounding gel coat will be quite thin, so avoid excessive zeal when rubbing it down. A piece of abrasive paper around a block of wood is safer than a power sander. Wet-and-dry paper with a No. 400 grit should be suitable. It will leave a matte surface which can be polished with a mild rubbing compound, either by hand or with a wool cover over a powered disk.

Resin mixtures have little strength or solidity by themselves to be used to build up thickness. In particular, polyester will *craze*: when fully cured, fine hairlike lines will appear in thick, unreinforced pieces. Because of this, damage that goes deeply into layers of glass should be filled (if wide enough) with strands of glass.

Scrape within the damaged area, preferably into the sides to provide some undercutting. Coat the inside of the hole with mixed resin, then press in pieces of glass fibers that have been teased out of a fiberglass mat or cloth. Fill with more resin. Press in hard enough to impregnate the fiberglass and squeeze out air bubbles. Make sure all of the glass is below the final surface. (The glass fibers in the resin will prevent crazing.)

Alternatively, there are resin putties available with finely chopped fiberglass already mixed in, which are suitable for these open repairs. Some marketed for automotive body repairs (the resin bonds to metal) are also suitable for boats.

Repairs as described will set with an off-white or pale brown color. As already stated, it is almost impossible to match colors exactly, but if you wish to make the repair less obvious, color pigment may be added to the mix before application.

Sometimes a scratch will go so deeply as to penetrate the hull's skin. If it was caused by rubbing against a sharp object without heavy impact, the scratch can be treated without having to cut the area any larger. If there was an impact that caused a crack away from the scratch, it will have to be treated as a major repair. If the cause of the damage is unknown, pushing or thumping around the area will disclose any cracks or other damage radiating from the scratch. If there are no signs of damage other than the scratch, proceed as follows:

Scrape out the groove. If it shows on the inside of the hull as a fine hairline, a better repair will be made if it is scraped to a greater width—say about ⅛ in.—on the inside and sanded to overlap the opening by about 1½ in. Do this only just before making the repair, so a perfectly new surface is presented to the patch. Cut a piece of fiberglass mat or cloth, or use a suitable piece of tape to match the area. A single thickness should be enough for most jobs, but if the crack is extensive and appears to need more support, a second, slightly smaller patch should be prepared. Have some loose strands of fiberglass ready for the crack if you are not using a resin containing chopped fiberglass.

Mix the resin and catalyst according to the supplier's directions. Apply some quickly with a brush on the inside, put the fiberglass patch over it, and impregnate it with resin by using the brush with a stippling or daubing action. Add more resin (with a stippling action) so the fiberglass is buried in the resin and there are no air bubbles. If a second layer is needed, it can follow in the same way—preferably immediately, although it will still bond satisfactorily after the first layer has cured.

This completes the work on the inside, but watch for running resin before it gels; covering it with cellophane may help. Examine the outside; if an excess of resin has worked through to the surface above, clean it away or press it into the crack.

Once the resin on the inside has reached the gel stage or has hardened, the crack may be filled from the outside in the same way described for a simple surface scratch. But use plenty of strands of fiberglass in the deeper parts of the groove to provide ample reinforcement. As before, make sure no air bubbles remain. Coloring may be filled to near the surface with uncolored resin and fiberglass threads, and a colored mixture applied as a final coat. The final coat should be leaving it slightly higher than the surrounding surface to allow for finish leveling (Fig. 3-1).

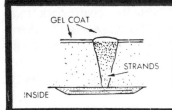

Fig. 3-1. The cross section of a fiberglass repair. A raised area is left on the outside to allow for final finishing.

## MAJOR REPAIRS

Fortunately, fiberglass will withstand considerable hard use and rough treatment, but heavy impacts with sharp obstructions will cause not only a puncture, but spreading cracks as well. When this happens, cut away the damaged area and replace it with new material rather than attempt to push cracked parts back into place. It is almost impossible to seal cracks and bond their edges together adequately without putting more resin on the outside and destroying the smooth lines of the hull. If the edges are not properly covered and sealed, there is a risk that water will seep into the material by capillary action.

The area is cut away to any outline that will clear the damage. There is no need for straight edges, but if the cutout is rectangular, it is better to avoid the abruptness of angles by rounding the corners (Fig. 3-2A). A saber saw is convenient for this, but it is possible to use a piece of hacksaw blade in a handle, or a fine-toothed keyhole saw. The edge of the opening should be prepared by filing. A disk sander might be used, but hand filing affords more control. How the edge is prepared depends on its thickness. If it is ⅛ in. or less, as in the average dinghy, the edge should be given a slight bevel toward the outside (Fig. 3-2B). Thicker material requires a double bevel (Fig. 3-2C). This is done to provide a foothold for the new resin.

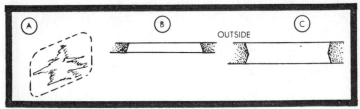

Fig. 3-2. Cutting techniques for removing a section of damaged hull prior to patching and filling. Different hull thicknesses require special cutout beveling.

If it is possible to get at both sides of the repair, work from the inside. If the boat can be tilted, get it into a position where the repair will be as nearly horizontal as possible. Gravity will help the flow of the resin. If the work has to be done vertically, it may be necessary to add thixotropic resin to the ordinary resin to reduce the risk of running.

If the curvature of the hull is moderate, a piece of cardboard, Masonite, or plywood may be used outside as a mold. This should be faced with cellophane and held to the hull with masking tape (Fig. 3-3A). If a piece of glossy, coated plywood can be obtained it can be coated with release compound and used without cellophane. If the backing piece is sufficiently flexible and only overlaps the opening by a small amount, the tape will hold it adequately. Additional pressure may be obtained by tying rope around the hull and using wedges (Fig. 3-3B).

If the curve to be followed is great, or the area of repair large, drill the hull and the backing piece, and pull the board tight with small nuts and bolts (Fig. 3-3C). Later the bolt holes can be filled with a resin and chopped fiberglass putty.

If possible, match the repair to the hull by using similar layers of fiberglass. By examining the hull, or the waste material cut out of it, it is possible to discover how many layers of fiberglass were used, which were woven cloth, and which were chopped strands. Cut enough pieces of similar

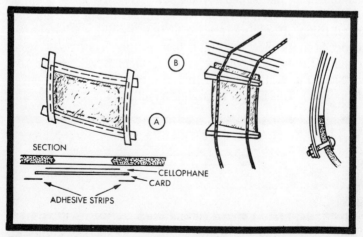

Fig. 3-3. Methods of holding a fiberglass mold against the hull.

material to make a reasonable fit in the hole. Cut more pieces large enough to overlap all around the inside. For a small job where the hole is not much more than an inch or so across, an overlap of an inch should be sufficient; but for larger areas, make it up to 2 in. Do all of this before preparing the resin. Trimming fiberglass to shape over wet resin would be messy and unsatisfactory. When the preliminaries are completed, use a disk sander or sandpaper and block on the inside surface, covering an area that includes the overlap.

First prepare just enough resin for the application of a gel coat on the inside of the cellophane. Make sure resin meets the cut edges of the hull. Let the resin become tacky; most mixes take about ten minutes or so, depending on temperature. Follow with more resin and layers of mat. Use the brush with a daubing or stippling action as each layer is applied and make sure the piece of mat is thoroughly wetted and there is no trapped air before applying the next layer. The job can continue right through until the overlapping pieces are fixed. However, it will not matter if you have to pause and continue again after a lower layer has gelled or even set completely. How many thicknesses of overlapping pieces of fiberglass are put inside will depend on circumstances. A small repair in a light hull may be sufficiently reinforced with one layer. The replacement of a large section of hull in a heavier craft could require three layers, each extending by a different amount.

Leave the completed job to cure; the resin maker will indicate how long this should be, but normally, overnight (at room temperature) will be long enough. Remove the cardboard or other mold piece from the outside and peel off the cellophane. In many cases the new surface may be good enough without further treatment. If there are defects in the surface, apply more resin, let it cure, then sand and polish it level with the old surface. Although resin cures comparatively quickly, its hardness increases over several days. If you are in no great hurry to do the final finishing immediately, you can achieve better results if you wait for this complete hardening.

Some parts of a boat have a compound curvature that prohibits the use of the mold pieces so far described. In these areas they cannot be shaped to form a close fit or give an outline of the correct shape. In such a case it is better to work from the outside. Trim and bevel the edges of the cutout as already described and sand around the inside to allow for overlapping patches. Woven fiberglass cloth will hold its shape better than chopped strand mat in this kind of work. Cut two cloth patches for the inside. Tilt the boat, if possible, the resin on top of the work. Thoroughly wet the patches with resin while they are on a cellophane-covered bench. Also apply a little resin around the inside of the cutout surfaces where the patches will go. Put both patches in place, pressing them down and daubing them with a brush. Manipulate them to conform to the desired shape. This can be done with a brush in one hand and a disposable plastic glove over the other.

Let the assembly cure. Cut fiberglass pieces to fit the hole, preferably of the same number and type as in the original construction. Tilt the work if possible, to keep the resin in place. Apply layers of resin and fiberglass, using the brush to wet each layer and drive out any air. Continue this process until you almost reach the final outline. This is difficult, but it is better to finish too thick than too thin. Apply a piece of cellophane over the outside, smoothing the surface with the hand, a roller, or a flat squeegee if there is little curvature involved. Then let the whole thing cure.

Next, use a disk sander or file to clean off the outside of the repair to very slightly below the intended finishing line. This area will be covered with a gel coat, as it is important that no fiberglass strands be exposed on the surface. Because the gel coat can be no more than a thin wash, the sanded surface must be almost the final shape; so if necessary build up the repair with resin and chopped fiberglass putty.

When you are satisfied with the shape, apply a layer of resin with a brush. Avoid reworking the brush over the same part too often. A perfect finish will not be obtained right off; it must be left to gel and cure first. The resin cannot be smoothed out like paint, but smoothing cellophane over the surface can help. Sand-polish the hardened surface to match the surrounding parts.

A different problem occurs when the inside is only accessible through the hole in the damaged area. The work obviously has to be done from outside; so how are the overlapping patches applied inside? By a special method: a backing piece is passed through the hole. To allow room for this, the area has to be trimmed to leave a hole considerably longer than it is wide. The length of the opening should be at least as much as the width plus an allowance for inside overlaps. The backing piece and patch will then go through and be turned to match up with the hole.

If the damage is to a panel that is nearly flat, the backing piece may be thin marine-grade plywood or Masonite. If not, the backing piece has to be more flexible, like cardboard, plastic, or even sheet metal. Once the fiberglass has set, the backing piece is of no further use; but because it cannot be removed, consideration must be given to what may happen to it. If cardboard is used, it will eventually disintegrate or become pulpy—which could block a bilge pump.

Trim the hole to shape and bevel the edges. Sand inside by reaching through with a piece of abrasive paper. Run pieces of copper or other saltwater-resistant wire through holes in the backing piece (Fig. 3-4A). For a small repair, one doubled wire will do, but more wires have to be used for a large piece or if there is much of a curve in the surface. The wire will be used to pull the backing and patches against the inside of the repair.

Put down two or more layers of cloth or mat and plenty of resin on the backing piece, leaving the wires standing up through them (Fig. 3-4B). Pass the assembly through the hole

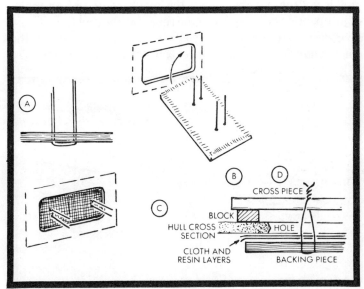

Fig. 3-4. Repairing a damaged area that is only accessible from the outside. A patch and backing piece must be passed through the hole and pulled against the inside.

and use the wires to turn and pull it into place (Fig. 3-4C). Have some blocks ready to support cross pieces, around which the wires will be tightened with pliers (Fig. 3-4D). When the assembly is secure, leave this to cure. After a sufficient amount of drying time, cut off the wire ends close to the resin. From this stage on, the repair is completed in the same way described for making an outside repair.

Some repairs are better made with a prefabricated section, rather than building it up at the site of the damage. Such a repair might involve an angular section in the bottom of the boat or the corner of a cabin top.

As before, the area is cut away and the edges are beveled. Although procedure will help determine the size of the replacement part to be made, the part should be large enough to overlap a little to permit trimming to fit.

A mold has to be made. This may call for some ingenuity, but except for the surfaces in contact with the part to be made, it can be quite crude. For the corner of a cabin top, pieces of plywood or Masonite, slightly oversize for the repair, are held together with blocks of wood to give the general outline. Curves are put in with modeling clay (Fig. 3-5A). For most jobs it will be possible to try the mold in position to make adjustments. Mark the size of the repair on the mold.

Brush the mold with two coats of release compound. If the compound is unavailable, use a good wax polish. Cut pieces of

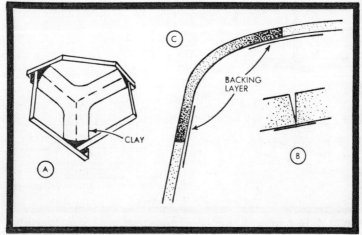

Fig. 3-5. Fiberglass repairs to angular boat sections necessitate the making of molds.

fiberglass to fit the repair. If there is much shaping to do, overlap the pieces. (Chopped strand mat is easier to shape than woven cloth.)

It does not matter if the prefabricated piece extends over the marked shape or has ragged edges. Apply resin liberally to the mold. When it begins to gel, put down the pieces of fiberglass, using the brush and more resin, pushing the material firmly into any curves. Smaller pieces of fiberglass may be worked into tighter curves. Build up the repair to about the same thickness as the original part, then remove the assembly after the resin has cured.

When the part has set sufficiently to be handled, but is not fully hard, it will be possible to cut the material with a knife or scissors. Otherwise, the finished piece may be sawed and filed to shape. There is no need for a precision fit—it is better, in fact, if there is a gap to allow resin to seep through (Fig. 3-5B) for a firmer hold.

Fix the prefabricated piece with backing layers of fiberglass that overlap inside on the sanded area around the original part (Fig. 3-5C). Don't be afraid to let resin come through the joint; it can be filed later before the new part is polished to match the old.

## POLISHES

A fiberglass hull as it comes from the manufacturer will have as good a gloss on it as the surface of the mold in which it was made—usually pretty good. But although the resin used is remarkably strong when reinforced with fiberglass, it does not have a very hard surface and can be easily scratched and dulled by anything mildly abrasive. If the hull has not been painted fairly early in its life, something of the original gloss can be revived with polishes.

Polishing fiberglass—like polishing anything else, is a matter of breaking down the surface with successively finer abrasives. Each polishing stage leaves finer scratches in the surface as it removes those from an earlier abrasive. Eventually a stage is reached when the scratches are too fine to be seen and we regard the surface as polished. Fortunately, with the comparatively soft resin, rubbing down in stages does not call for an excessive amount of hard work; only the gel coat is polished, and it may be but a few thousandths of an inch thick. Hard rubbing, especially with a power polisher, may cause you to go right through it. If strands of glass are exposed, you will be faced with a minor repair. Consequently, it is wiser to confine fiberglass polishing to hand work.

There are many fiberglass polishes on the market, but most of them are finishing polishes. If the surface is so badly abraded that there is a general matte effect with scratches clearly visible, rubbing with a finishing polish would be a lengthy job. If this sort of surface has to be brought to a gloss again, something coarser is needed at first: pumice powder or a household cleaner on a wet cloth. Use plenty of powder with a scouring action, wash it off, and dry the surface.

This is followed with a cutting compound used normally on automobile bodies. Another suitable compound is sold for removing scratches from plastic windows. This stage may be regarded as intermediate; and all traces of the compound used must be removed before moving on to the final polishing.

Most polishes sold for fiberglass contain solvents for dirt and grease, so they clean as well as shine. A wax polish provides much more than a shiny appearance; it provides a film of protection that will resist those things in the air and water which cause dulling.

## SURFACE PREPARATION

If the paint on a surface is to last as long as possible, each coat must adhere to the one below it, and the bottom coat to the base material. If there is any contamination of the base material with grease or dirt, the first coat will merely cover the dirty film; and the strength of the paint job will depend on the adhesion to the contamination. The paint will fail and break away after a short time. Apart from other considerations, good paint is expensive to waste in this way.

These considerations apply to any material, but the porosity of wood, cement, and some other materials allows paint to penetrate and get a grip, even in the presence of some contamination. The gel coat on a fiberglass hull is hardly porous at all. Everything must be done to insure a clean surface before painting.

Among the contaminants that have to be dealt with are: the mold release compounds that remain on the hull long after manufacture; the oils that float on the water and wash over a large part of the boat; and the waxes used during the period leading up to the painting. All of these must be removed completely before painting. A glossy surface, even when it is clean, does not form a good base for paint—so preparation involves *removing gloss* as well as contamination.

The first step in cleaning a fiberglass surface is to use a stiff brush and a strong solution of powdered detergent. Work systematically to give all parts a really hard rubbing. Release compound tends to last longest in hollows and grooves; make sure you get to the bottom of them. When you have done this, remove all traces of detergent with plenty of fresh water; then let the surface dry.

The next step is sanding, particularly if any gloss remains. Do the sanding by hand with a fine grade of wet-and-dry abrasive paper (3/0 or 120 grit) wrapped around a block of wood. Power sanding might go through the gel coat. After sanding, the surface should look so dull that it will reflect practically no light.

The last stage in preparation is wiping with a solvent. This can be mineral spirits or the solvent recommended by the paint manufacturer. Use a cloth, refolding it frequently to maintain a clean surface during use.

## PAINTING FIBERGLASS

A fiberglass boat has color included in the molding and should retain a fairly even color throughout its life as long as it remains in good condition, particularly if the color goes right through. Less commonly, the color may only be in the gel coat or outlayers of resin. It would be rather idealistic to believe that this sort of coloring is durable. Usually, by the time a hull needs repairing it will have become generally shabby and an overall paint job is called for; a molded cabin top may retain its appearance for a long time, but the hull takes knocks and becomes scratched. Even mild abrasion will produce discrepancies in the basic color. And when repairs have to be made, it is almost impossible to match colors with pigments; a repair which is slightly off-color will look as bad as one where no attempt was made to color it.

The early extravagant claims of some manufacturers that fiberglass never needs painting have been proved wrong by experience, and some owners now feel that there is a case for painting a fiberglass hull long before it becomes shabby. There are now several synthetic paints which will give a good durable finish to fiberglass. Several layers of paint provide protection from abrasion and minor knocks. A chipped paint surface is much easier to touch up than a damaged gel coat.

The mechanics of applying paint are described in elsewhere; here we are concerned with the choice and planning of a *paint system* for fiberglass. It is best to stay with the products of one paint manufacturer and follow his advice. Most manufacturers will also provide booklets describing the application of their products. Anyone with experience in using paints common a few years ago will find that some of the modern synthetics require rather different treatment; it is wise to read thoroughly any instructions provided with the paint.

Most paint manufacturers supply a special primer for fiberglass. This may be a one-pot paint, or it may be a formulation similar to the molding resin (requiring that a hardener be added just before use and that the paint be applied within a certain time limit). Another requirement with some fiberglass primers is that they are only allowed a limited time (2 or 3 hours) to dry before the paint coat is applied.

Modern paints are known by trade manes. This may be just as well for the nontechnical amateur, since the chemical names may add to his confusion. A few generic terms for fiberglass applications are: silicon alkyd, acrylic, epoxy, and polyurethane. Some of these are only suitable for professional application under controlled conditions with special spray equipment. For brush application by amateurs, silicon alkyds give good results. Polyurethane and epoxy also brush well on fiberglass. The two-part types give the most durable finish, but a one-pot version can also give a satisfactory finish.

The primer provides special treatment for the fiberglass. What follows it is a matter of choice; probably it will be the same as that used on other materials—providing the manufacturer agrees that the primer is compatible with it. For some finishes there is an undercoat which dries to a matte finish that is followed by a final glossy coat. With some makes of paint it is recommended that both coats be the same. An enamel or gloss finish is applied and allowed to dry overnight, then it is lightly sanded and a further coat of the same paint is applied to finish the job.

Some finishing paints are suitable for direct application to fiberglass without the use of a primer. One of these is *silicon copolymer*, although it needs a primer if it is to be used on other materials. The tightest direct bond to fiberglass is claimed for catalyzed epoxy (i. e., epoxy paint with a catalyst or hardener added before use).

## NONSLIP FIBERGLASS

The usual method of forming fiberglass in a mold produces a high gloss in fiberglass, which is what is wanted for most parts of a boat. However, decks need to be given a finish without gloss to provide a grip for shoes. Obviously, prevention of slipping on a deck is a prime safety requirement. Unfortunately, merely sanding the surface will not do. The outer layer of a normal fiberglass molding is a comparatively thin resin coat; if it is rubbed through and some of the fiberglass exposed, moisture will enter. There are treatments used during manufacture that produce a nonslip surface. Sometimes a nonslip pattern is molded in for the same effect.

Eventually, manufactured nonslip treatments deteriorate. This is often about the time the hull becomes shabby and an all-over paint job is advisable. However, if ordinary paint is applied to a nonslip surface, it will destroy any remaining grip. Something else is called for.

There are self-adhesive, nonslip plastic strips which can be stuck on. These are useful for parts of side decks that are exposed to heavy traffic. They can be arranged in a pattern over large areas, but they are more suitable for smaller spaces. To get the best adhesion, the deck must be prepared as if it was to be painted. Dirt and grease have to be removed with abrasive powder or solvent. When the deck is absolutely dry, lightly pencil a few key marks where a strip is to go; adhesion is lessened if a strip has to be lifted to be repositioned. Remove the backing from a strip, fix one end on the deck, then lower the rest into place while stroking away from the fixed end to work out air bubbles. Maintain a slight stretch as the strip is fitted. If, despite all your care, there is an air bubble which cannot be worked out towards an edge, prick its center with a needle to let the air out, then press the strip flat.

If a deck has to be painted, either for general appearance or to disguise a repair, there is no reason not to use a nonskid additive with the paint.

A deck will need the same system as a hull, with a primer where appropriate. If the top coat is to be a conventional paint, it should be one that dries to a matte or semigloss finish. Fine sand can be mixed with the paint just before application, if you keep the paint stirred as the job proceeds. Beach sand should be avoided because the salt in it may affect the paint. Sand from a building supplier is most suitable. How much sand you use is a matter of experience and preference, rather than exact specification. Experiment on a small area and let it dry before doing the whole deck.

Although sand should work successfully with any paint, it would be wiser to accept the paint maker's advice about the special paints for fiberglass. If the paint for the deck has to match the color of some other part that is not required to have a nonslip finish, it would be easier to use the same paint throughout. Most marine paint manufacturers supply either a paste or powder to give their paints nonslip qualities.

## JOINING OTHER MATERIALS TO FIBERGLASS

When making repairs or alterations to a boat it may be necessary to add or refix such things as wooden bulkheads and metal fittings. Fortunately, the joints involved will present no difficulties.

In general, fiberglass-reinforced plastic has sufficient strength in comparatively thin sections, particularly if the design uses plenty of curves to add stiffness. Boat parts designed to be built from this material are very seldom flat, or near flat, and will almost certainly contain no abrupt angles. The material will also be easier to work with, and will be ultimately stronger, if it is not used to embrace sharp angles. These characteristics should be remembered when altering or adding to a fiberglass boat.

Although curves will enhance the stiffness of a panel, there will not be much local strength; a cleat, for instance, might be very securely attached to a fiberglass deck or hull, but a load on it might distort the material if nothing was done to spread the load. For a lightly loaded part, it might be permissible to merely install fixing bolts, but even then there should be large

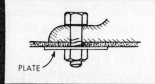

PLATE

Fig. 3-6. A plate can be used to reinforce the fiberglass panel in the area of the fixing bolt.

washers or a specially drilled plate on the opposite side (Fig. 3-6) to give a large load-bearing surface.

This method, however, is not advisable in many situations, even for something normally lightly loaded. If a hook is grabbed by someone with a boathook to stop the boat in a lock, the fasteners might break away a portion of the molding. If the method is used, embed the fitting in molding resin or a joining compound and coat the fixing bolts with resin. This prevents water from seeping through and serves to lock the nut on each bolt (although it can still be removed with a wrench).

Where more strength is needed, mold in a reinforcing wood block (Fig. 3-7). This should be a good piece of durable hardwood or strong, marine-grade plywood, not just any odd piece of lumber that happens to be around. Avoid the "greasy" woods, such as teak.

The wood should extend around the base of the fitting, or the location of the fixing screws, by several inches. How far it extends and how thick it should be will depend on the load involved. A reinforcement intended to take the load of a mooring cleat on a foredeck obviously needs to be larger and stronger than one used to back up a coat hook on a cabin bulkhead. A typical size for the former application might be 8 in. square and 1 in. thick, while the latter could be 3 in. square and ⅜ in. thick. If there is any curve to be matched, the wood should be shaped to make a reasonable fit, although minor imperfections will be taken care of when the wood is in place.

A reinforcing piece may be rectangular, but the corners should be rounded and the edges beveled to about 45° (Fig. 3-7A). Drill small pilot holes through the fiberglass for the fixing bolts. These serve two purposes: They show you the location of the job inside; and they allow temporary woodscrews to be used to hold the reinforcing block while the resin sets. Using the holes as a guide, mark the area where the

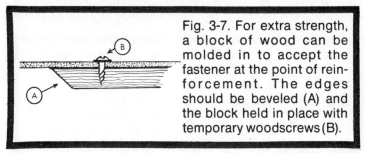

Fig. 3-7. For extra strength, a block of wood can be molded in to accept the fastener at the point of reinforcement. The edges should be beveled (A) and the block held in place with temporary woodscrews (B).

wood is to go; then use a sander to break through the old surface inside and to expose a new matte surface just before attaching the wood. Sand several inches outside the area for the wood.

Coat the surface of wood and fiberglass to be joined with resin. This will be sufficient if the wood makes a close fit. Otherwise, apply one or two layers of chopped strand mat and resin to the wood before the joint is made. While an assistant holds it in place, drive temporary woodscrews, with washers under the heads, through from outside (Fig. 3-7B).

When the resin has gelled, or completely hardened (if there is no hurry), apply more fiberglass and resin, daubing the brush. Use plenty of resin. If you are working overhead, use a thixotropic resin to lessen the risk of having it come away while liquid. How the fiberglass is cut depends on the shape of the reinforcement, but a convenient way is to use strips extending a short distance from each side of the wood (Fig. 3-8A). Because the wood is beveled and rounded, the fiberglass should conform to it quite well, but work out any air bubbles by stippling with the brush. Try to completely enclose the wood. When the whole assembly has set, remove the screws and enlarge the holes to take fixing bolts. Even with a wood reinforcement it is advisable—and good engineering—to use large washers or a specially drilled plate under the bolts (Fig. 3-8B).

The same idea may be used in special situations. The wood might have to fit into the rounded corner. In that case, besides fitting the edge of the wood to the curve, an angled molding strip will have to be included so the fiberglass can be laid on without having to conform to a sharp angle (Fig. 3-9).

If the block is completely enclosed in fiberglass-reinforced resin, it does not have to make an absolutely perfect bond with the resin. In fact, the resins themselves, both epoxy and polyester, will act as strong wood glues. If something like a

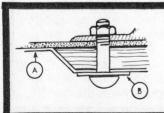

Fig. 3-8. After the resin has hardened, the woodscrews are removed, fiberglass applied (A), and fixing bolts put in with washers or a specially drilled plate (B).

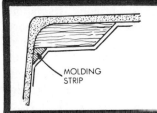

Fig. 3-9. To avoid having to make the fiberglass conform to a sharp angle, a strip of molding (fillet) is used in the corner.

MOLDING STRIP

plywood bulkhead in a cruiser, or a wooden seatback in a runabout, has to be attached to a fiberglass hull, the attachment is more like gluing because most of the wood will not be enclosed.

Plywood bulkheads may be reinforced with a double thickness, or be merely reinforced on one side. It should be sanded to a clean, matte surface for several inches on each side of the area to be joined. The shape of the bulkhead may be derived by spiling, but it should not be cut for a forced fit. Bulkheads or any other transverse item in a hull, when forced in, may seem satisfactory at first. But after some time its position will be noticed from the outside as sunlight coming from certain directions disclosed by distortions in the surface. The higher the gloss, the more apparent this will be. It is better to fit the bulkhead somewhat loosely—say ⅛ in. too small all around; but such precision can be difficult with a rather involved shape (Fig. 3-10A).

Position the bulkhead with temporary bracing, preferably all on one side. On the other side, use resin and tape, or strips of cloth, joining the bulkhead and hull (Fig. 3-10B). Two thicknesses should be laid. Try to impregnate all of the fiberglass with resin; if some of it seeps through the weave of the cloth, it won't matter at this stage.

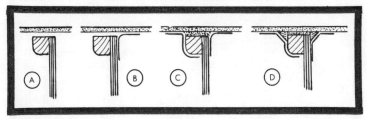

Fig. 3-10. To install a bulkhead, it is first braced just near the hull (A); joined with tape (B); the space filled in with fiberglass and the block covered (C). The joint can be additionally strengthened with triangular fillets (D).

When the resin has set, remove the bracing. Use small pieces of fiberglass and resin to fill the space between the edge of the bulkhead and the hull. This is an opportunity to use up scrap pieces because almost any form of fiberglass will do. Having done this, preferably while the resin was still soft, apply an additional thickness or two of tape to form a fillet (molding strip) on the other side (Fig. 3-10C). Packing from the back will probably have filled any holes in the first tape, but if any remain, fill them now. If the contour of the job allows it, use small triangular fillets to improve the joints by removing the abrupt angles (Fig. 3-10D).

The same methods can be used for other interior fittings. For some jobs, a combination of techniques is best. For instance, if the supports for a cockpit or cabin have to be attached to the hull, the load will be better distributed if lengthwise battens (strips of wood) are molded to the hull (Fig. 3-11A) in the same way described for reinforcing; then the supports are laid on the battens and are held by blocks of wood screwed in place (Fig. 3-11B) and covered with fiberglass. A shelf or bunk top may also be fixed in this way. Attaching it like a bulkhead would not provide adequate security under violent loads. In this case, it is better to bond supports to the hull and fix the top to them (Fig. 3-11C).

Cable steering can put considerable strain on the attachments for the pulleys, particularly when the helmsman finds it necessary to turn the helm hard. Neither woodscrews and reinforcing blocks nor bolting methods are able to stand up to the strains imposed. If broken or worn fastenings have to be repaired, the reinforcing blocks will have to be enlarged and stiffening pieces put on the transom to share the load (Fig.

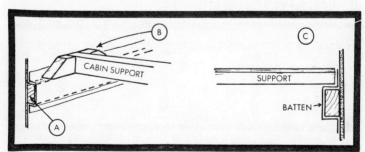

Fig. 3-11. Fitting supports for other structures. A batten (A) is fixed to the hull, to which blocks (B) are screwed to hold the support; the same method can be used for shelves (C).

78

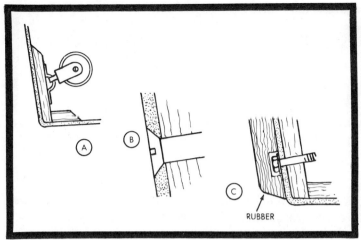

Fig. 3-12. (A) How to best spread the load on a cable pulley. A countersunk bolt head (B) can be easily disguised, but this is not the strongest arrangement. It is better to let the head protrude; then it can be covered with rubber as a bumper (C).

3-12A). The pulley fittings should be attached with bolts going right through all sections. Heads showing on the outside of a hull are certainly unattractive. They could be countersunk and disguised with resin or paint (Fig. 3-12B), but then they wouldn't spread the load as well as desired. It is better to use some form of raised head with a washer under it. This can be disguised with a quarter rubber—a small bumper that is seamanlike in any case (Fig. 3-12C)—to protect the corners of the transom from knocks.

In general, it is advisable to avoid trying to bond metal to fiberglass. It is better to use bolts, as already described. However, there are occasions when something like an embedded bolt head with a projecting thread can be used as a stud for making attachments. The bolt head can fit directly against the deck or hull (Fig. 3-13A), or some wood reinforcement may be added (Fig. 3-13B). The embedded bolt will better resist turning under the torque of a tightened nut if it has a hexagonal or square head.

Nearly all metal objects come from the manufacturer with a slightly greasy surface. This would resist resin bond and must be removed. Degreasing agents and many paint solvents will work. But in their absence, scrub the part with strong

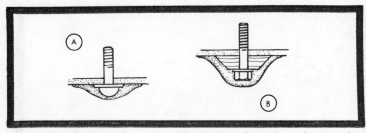

Fig. 3-13. A protruding bolt shank can be a handy attachment point. The head can fit flush (A) or be reinforced (B).

detergent, rinse it with clear water, and allow it to dry completely. Avoid handling the surface to be bonded after this stage because the grease from your hands will affect bonding.

Polyester resin does not bond very well to metal of any sort. Epoxy is very much better. A metal part may be bonded entirely with epoxy, but this would be expensive; an alternative is to coat the metal with epoxy and let it gel or completely harden, then complete the bonding with polyester resin. How the job is done depends on circumstances and purpose.

# Woodworking

4

The Vikings built their longboats with overlapping planks; the method, known variously as lapstraking and clinker-building, produced light craft that were strong enough to make Atlantic crossings. This construction technique is still in use today, although obviously it has had to give way to alternative, more modern methods in many places. Emigrants carried the method to America. Boatbuilders in the Scandinavian countries, and to a lesser extent in Britain and North America, may still be found building small craft, lifeboats, whaleboats and small cruisers in this way.

The overlaps of planks in boats built by this traditional method do not have any jointing material and depend on the tightness of fastenings and the swelling of wood when it gets wet. Consequently, such a boat is best kept afloat, or at least not allowed to dry out completely. An old boat that has been brought ashore and left exposed to the sun for a long period may never fully tighten again. However, if such a boat swells almost as soon as it is put afloat, it should not be condemned as being beyond hope. It is surprising how much the wood will "take up" after a thorough soaking. If the boat can be left at the bottom of a ramp, where it is allowed to float for a few hours on each tide, in two weeks any leaks will become manageable, even if the hull is not completely tight.

A lapstrake boat in good condition can be very attractive. New boats of varnished mahogany have a beauty unobtainable by most other building methods. If such a boat has to be repaired, the easy way out is to fill any hole with fiberglass. But it is much more satisfactory to make the repair in the traditional way. This involves some woodworking skill, but a capacity for taking care is more important than a high degree of craftsmanship.

## MINOR REPAIRS

Wood, being a natural product derived from a variety of trees with their attendant differences in characteristics, can have many forms with differences in strength, hardness, weight, and stiffness. Some woods, such as *lignum vitae*, are very hard and unlikely to be damaged, while at the other extreme are the spruces, which have value in lightness with strength for spars and other shipboard purposes, but are very susceptible to minor damage. Between these are the popular boatbuilding woods, such as mahogany and teak, both remarkably tough and durable, but still liable to surface damage.

Scratches and abrasion are of little consequence to the oilier woods, like teak, which are unlikely to absorb much water even when not protected by paint. Spruce and other light-colored softwoods can absorb a considerable amount of water through exposed grain. This adds weight and may promote rotting. Once the water is absorbed, it takes a long time to dry out; it travels by capillary action along the grain under the paint or varnish. The moral here is: carry some quick-drying varnish to dab over damage before water has a chance to enter. Varnished mahogany gives any boat a smart appearance, but if water gets below the varnish, the wood turns gray and the discoloration shows through the varnish. Nothing much can be done about this. If the varnish is removed, it is possible to bleach the gray wood before revarnishing, but the result is likely to be imperfect; there will still be unevenness in the appearance.

Minor lifting of the grain can be dealt with by sanding. Hand sanding is preferable to using a power sander. A power sander may be too powerful and remove more wood than you intended. A disk sander will make scratches across the grain, which will have to be removed by hand before varnishing. A medium grade of abrasive paper is probably all that is needed, although a finer grade works better on harder woods. Attempting to use too fine a grade on soft woods only results in grit clogging the wood and the paper becoming useless before it has had much effect.

Use folded abrasive paper in the hand for shaped parts, but for flat and moderately curved surfaces, wrap it around a block. Tearing a sheet (usually 9 in. by 11 in.) into four is a convenient and economical way of working when used with a block about 4 inches by 3 inches by 1¼ inches. This may be a piece of wood, but traditionally a block of cork was claimed by woodworking craftsman to have special texture properties to suit the job. It is a fact that it is better to support the paper with a surface slightly softer than the wood to be sanded. An alternative to cork is a wood block faced with hard rubber.

Straightforward dry sanding will produce a good surface on hardwoods, but softwood fibers sometimes have a tendency to bend over rather than rub off. Sand softwoods both ways with the grain, then brush the surface and wipe it with a damp cloth. This will raise any bent fibers. When the water has evaporated, sand again to remove the raised fibers.

If cracks or scratches have to be filled, or plugs over screw heads replaced, use a plastic-wood filler. Some of these fillers are made for cabinetwork and may not be waterproof. For boat work, be careful to select one that is marked *waterproof*. These compounds set without shrinking and can be obtained in several colors to match many woods. When the compound is set, the surface is worked like the surrounding wood. Consequently, it is possible to leave some above the surface and sand it flush after it sets.

Because wood-plastic fillers set hard, they are unsuitable for places that have to expand and contract. Small fillings in the usual boatbuilding hardwoods will be subjected to variations too small to bother about. Sometimes in softwoods, however, expansion and contraction are greater around a large crack. In *lapstrake planking* there may be spaces between planks which never completely swell to fit. If a hard filling is used in an attempt to fill such a gap, further swelling against the hard material might cause a seam to open elsewhere. A solid pole used as a spar will almost certainly develop lengthwise cracks. These will not affect a spar's strength, but they may be unsightly enough to warrant filling. However, a hard filling might cause the crack to lengthen when the wood shrinks against it; or there might be gaps around it when the wood expands.

Waterproof puttylike compounds, often supplied in tubes or gun-type pressure applicators, are ideal for this sort of situation. The advantage of these materials is that they never completely harden; they will bond to the wood and move with it. The surface hardens to a seal that can be painted like the surrounding wood. Two-part epoxy calking compounds handle

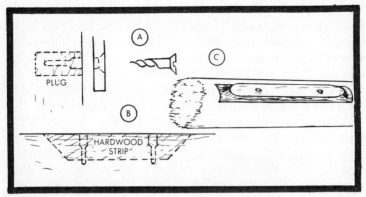

Fig. 4-1. Patching in plugs to accept fasteners. In single-screw applications, a hole is drilled for a hardwood plug; then the plug is drilled for the screw (A). For two or more screws, a strip is best (B); the strip can have a raised, flat surface if a cleat is to be mounted (C).

like putty, but set slightly flexible to allow for movement in the wood.

One minor problem, particularly with softwoods, is a screw that won't hold. Sometimes a slightly longer or thicker one has to be substituted. But if the same size screw has to be used, the hole should be filled with epoxy resin, or the screw dipped in epoxy before insertion; then the screw is clamped in place until the resin sets and bonds the wood to the metal.

An alternative to this is using one of the plugs sold for screws in masonry.

The woodworker's method of dealing with the problem is to plug in a piece of harder wood. A hole is drilled, a hardwood plug glued in, and a hole is drilled in the plug to take the screw (Fig. 4-1A). Although this idea works for single screws, if the job involves a cleat or other thing with a base that takes two or more screws, it is better to patch in a beveled strip of hardwood (Fig. 4-1B). If it is a rounded spar, the inset can be made oversize and shaped to match after the glue has set, leaving a flat surface to match the cleat (Fig. 4-1C).

Using a piece of hardwood to strengthen a softwood part is good craftsmanship. Modern waterproof glues that set as strong as wood made this sort of reinforcing possible. They have also allowed wood to be laminated, where previously an article had to be carved from a solid piece—a wasteful procedure.

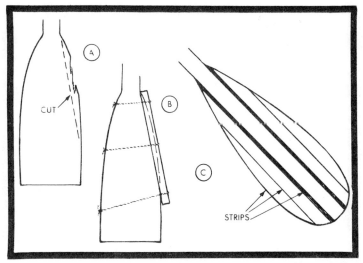

Fig. 4-2. Oar repair. A damaged edge is cut off straight, then an oversize piece is glued in place and trimmed to shape (A & B). If the damage is extensive, a new oar can be built up around the old shaft (C).

A good example for this process is a paddle (or oar blade). An edge that has been damaged is first cut off straight (Fig. 4-2A). Next, a piece of wood, bigger than finally needed, is glued and tied on (Fig. 4-2B); then it is trimmed to shape, resulting in a strong repair.

A complete blade can be built up on each side of the central shaft and stiffened with thin pieces of hardwood. Besides providing strength, the contrasting color of the hardwood makes the oar quite handsome (Fig. 4-2C).

Because glue does not bond well to end grain, when wood parts have to be lengthened, they should be *scarfed*: both pieces cut to matching angles and joined. The recommended angle is about 8°. But this can be derived without angular measurement by making the sloping, pointed section of the pieces seven times longer than their thickness (Fig. 4-3A). They can be beveled to match with a minimum of measuring and marking if they are clamped together with one set back from the end of the other to a distance equal to seven times the thickness (Fig. 4-3B). The pieces are then sawed along a line drawn across the points indicated in Fig. 4-3C, providing a perfect match. The pieces can be clamped to a bench and the two ends planed together. This sort of joint is best held while

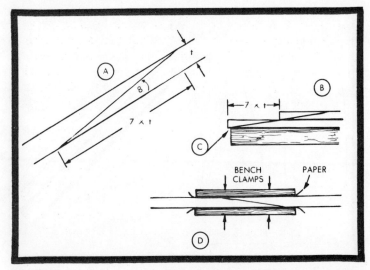

Fig. 4-3. Scarfing wood parts together. The ends of the parts are cut to matching angles and joined (A). The angle can be derived by staggering the parts by an amount equal to seven times their thickness (B). (Thickness = t.) The assembly is then planed between clamps protected from glue with paper (C).

the glue sets by clamping the ends between straight boards, with paper between them (Fig. 4-3D). The paper prevents the boards from sticking to the job when glue oozes out of the joint.

When repairing a shaped part, such as a spar or boathook shaft, it is advisable to use a new piece that is slightly oversize in cross section; It is not easy to get the parts joined exactly in line, this will allow enough leeway to shape the new piece to match the old one.

While working it to the final shape, sight along it often to make sure that the new piece is a true continuation. Glue makes a stronger joint when it's used on side grain rather than end grain; so whenever possible, a new piece to be inset should be beveled in a way that will avoid an end-grain joint.

If you're working with new wood that has been machine-planed, it is advisable to either hand plane the surface or thoroughly sand it. This is because the rotating planer blades may have been blunt. Blunted blades tend to pound the surface as well as cut it, causing it to become *case hardened*. This in effect closes the pores, preventing glue from being properly absorbed and resulting in a weak joint. If the area to be glued is comparatively small, it would also be worthwhile to scratch the matin surfaces to give the glue greater penetration and contact. This can be done with a knife or a spike, or by dragging handsaw teeth across it in several directions. Cracks or splits can often be dealt with by forcing glue into the crevices and clamping them shut while the glue sets. To get best glue penetration, spread the crack slightly and apply the glue with a disposable syringe.

Normally, wood glues lack the flexibility required for a spar or other piece that has cracked due to flexing. An alternative to gluing is to wrap the damaged area with fiberglass tape and epoxy resin (less rigid than polyester resin). More epoxy can be used to fill the crack. This is the sort of repair that can be part of preventive maintenance. For example, a spar can be bound in this manner to reinforce it at the point of greatest strain.

Screwing or nailing across a crack in a part subjected to strain must be tackled cautiously. The metal fasteners pull the parts together, but they may weaken the part by breaking away some of the fibers in the cross section.

## WOODWORKING TOOLS

Minor repairs to wooden boats can be made with the tools suggested for a basic kit, but there are many others worth having, to do the work better or more expeditiously. Many of the additional tools are really variations of, or different sizes of, the basic equipment. A really comprehensive tool kit makes possible more advanced woodworking repairs.

While nearly all sawing can be done with one general-purpose saw, finer work requires a saw with smaller teeth. The advantage: it is possible to cut much closer to the final size without risk of mistake; final planing or other finishing is reduced or made unnecessary. The saw most workers choose is a backsaw or tenon about 12 in. long with 16 teeth per inch. This is the most-used tool for precision cutting. If the line to be cut is marked with a knife instead of a pencil, and the saw is kept close to the waste side of the line, the finish will be exact and smooth.

A bench hook is a good companion for a tenon saw. This can be a homemade affair consisting of a small board with a stopping piece at one end, against which the work is pushed (one can be seen in Fig. 2-7) while sawing. It has uses with other tools when you need to hold wood against something.

A pad handle is of more use in boat repairing than most other woodworking. It can hold a hacksaw blade for cutting fastenings between planks and is much more efficient and comfortable than the more usual method of using a blade wrapped with electrician's tape. For this sort of work, turn the blade so it cuts on the pulling stroke. A pad handle with a narrow saw blade is convenient for cutting wood in confined spaces or close to curves. The handle can be used with other tools, such as small files. Some handles are specially designed to take both replaceable knife blades and saw blades. There are other knives on the market with multiple uses, intended for hunters and woodsmen. The saws in these combination tools are usually useless to a boat repairer.

A comparatively recent addition to the variety of saws available is a hole cutter. This device holds curved pieces of hacksaw blade, supplied in different diameters, and turned by a drill. Although intended for a power drill, they can be worked with a hand drill. In boat repairing they are valuable for breaking through damaged parts to view parts inside from outside, or vice versa. In this case, a ¼ in. drill is first used to make a starter hole. If examination shows this to be about right, a hole cutter follows. The hole produced then allows examination from either side and will be big enough to get a small saw or other tool through.

Jigsaws and saber saws, as well being useful for trimming down damaged parts, will also cut through copper or brass fastenings. They may be self-powered or attach to a portable drill. A table saw in the workshop is valuable for cutting wood to the required dimensions but so much of the wood in a boat is curved that it has less uses than might be expected. The workshop saw of greatest value to a boat repairer is the bandsaw. It works with more precision than a portable saber saw and will cut thicker wood.

The repairer faced with a variety of woodworking jobs often wishes for something just a little different from what he has in the way of cutting tools. This is reflected in the enormous range of chisels, planes, and similar tools being manufactured. General-purpose chisels are made in widths from ⅛ in. or less up to about 2 in. *Shipwright's chisels* were even wider. Sooner or later the woodworker will find that he is just making do with his one chisel when he really needs something narrower or wider. Chisels in all available widths

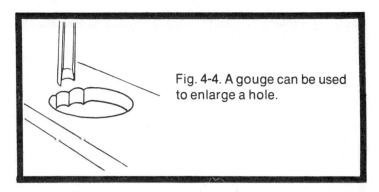

Fig. 4-4. A gouge can be used to enlarge a hole.

are a good investment, particularly the narrower ones. Most of the chisels should be bevel-edged; they will do all that a square-edged chisel will, and get into corners besides. Versions called *paring chisels* have longer and thinner blades. For trimming the taper in a section of new plank to be scarfed in, there is nothing like a broad paring chisel, say, 1½ in. to 2 in. wide.

Gouges are not so essential. They are made in general-purpose and paring types, like chisels, and are further complicated by being sharpened either inside or outside. A boat repairer might find a ½ in. general-purpose gouge sharpened on the inside useful for final shaping inside a curve. Suppose a piece of plywood has a hole to take a fitting and it is not quite big enough. The gouge can be used in a series of overlapping cuts to bring the edge to a new line (Fig. 4-4).

The smoothing and block planes suggested for the basic kit will take care of most planing requirements. If more planes are obtained, they should be longer. The longer the base, the easier it is to make a straight, flat surface. A plane of moderate length is called a jack plane; the name comes from "jack-of-all-trades," meaning general-purpose. A very long one is a *try*, or *jointer* plane. In boat work there is little use for the special planes for making grooves, unless you have to deal with internal cabinetwork. An exception is the replacement of lapstrake planking near one end of the boat where one plank has to be brought down to the level of another in a channel called a *rebate* (Fig. 4-5). The plane blade's full width is used to make the rebate. If this sort of job is anticipated, a rebate plane about 1 in. in width should be included in the repair kit.

Planes are available with throwaway blades. New blades are slid in, rather like replacing razor blades. They work quite

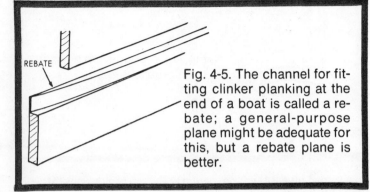

Fig. 4-5. The channel for fitting clinker planking at the end of a boat is called a rebate; a general-purpose plane might be adequate for this, but a rebate plane is better.

REBATE

well, and although an expert might not approve of them, they have their uses in repair work when sharpening facilities are not available.

Sharpening plane irons and chisels does not require much skill. With a little practice you will set a good edge. If an edge is examined in a cross light and a white line is seen as the metal reflects the light, the tool is blunt. A perfectly sharp tool has opposite surfaces meeting at an edge of no width, so there is nothing to reflect light. Absolute perfection may be impossible to attain, but aim to get somewhere near it.

Use a light oil on an *oilstone* held in a vice or pushed against a bench hook; leather or rubber glued to the bottom of the case will help make it nonslip for use almost anywhere. The tool to be sharpened has to be held so that its edge is parallel to the surface of the stone (Fig. 4-6A). Use both hands, one to push and control the angle. Spread the fingers of the other hand over the end to apply pressure (Fig. 4-6B). The tool has to be rubbed up and down the surface of the stone at a *constant* angle—this is where skill comes in. The natural inclination is to dip the hands and flatten the angle towards the far end of the stroke. This must be resisted and the angle maintained. There are roller devices to clamp the tool to maintain the angle, but most workers find they can manage without them.

The stone will wear away gradually. To keep the wear even and the surface flat, cover as much of the surface as possible when you use it. When you think you have rubbed enough, wipe the tool with a cloth. When the bevel has been rubbed sufficiently there will be a fine sliver of steel, called a *wire edge*, clinging to the edge and curled over (Fig. 4-6C). It

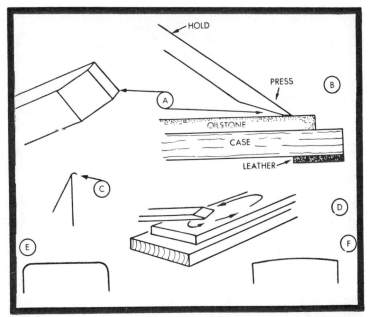

Fig. 4-6. Honing the cutting edges of planes and chisels (A) requires an oilstone, preferably with its case supported on leather to prevent slipping (B). The edge can only be considered sharp after a wire edge is formed (C) and rubbed off (D). Different planes have to have different bevels (E & F).

can always be felt as roughness when you rub a finger down the flat side of the blade towards the edge. If there is no wire edge, the tool cannot be considered adequately sharpened.

To remove the wire edge, rub the tool flat on the stone with a circular motion (Fig. 4-6D), then slice the edge across a piece of scrap wood. The tools is now ready for use. A plane iron can be prevented from digging-in and leaving ridges on a broad surface if the corners are rounded on the stone (Fig. 4-6E). A plane intended for the quick removal of a large amount of wood before fine planing should have an edge that looks slightly convex (Fig. 4-6F). How close the back iron is fitted in a plane depends on the wood to be cut or how coarse the cut is to be made. For fine finishing of hardwoods, the back iron should be less than $1/16$ in. from the blade edge; for coarse planing of softwoods, about $1/8$ in.

A piece of thin gouge to be sharpened on the inside requires an *oil slip*: a thin piece of oilstone with a rounded edge and used like a file. The wire edge that results is removed by

Fig. 4-7. Drill bits; from left to right: a center bit used in a hand brace for shallow holes; a similar bit designed for power drills; a wood bit for deep, power drilling; two bits for deep, hand drilling.

rubbing the convex side on a flat oilstone. Thin plane irons usually have edges with a single bevel; chisels usually have a compound bevel, i.e., two adjoining bevels, such as can be seen in Fig. 4-6A.

There is so much drilling that has to be done on a boat that it's just about impossible to have *too many* drill bits. A sampling of what might be needed is shown in Fig. 4-7. Small Morse-pattern drills are as effective on wood as on metal, and should be accumulated as the need for them arises. For larger holes spade-type bits for power drills are useful, especially if the wood is thin or the hole is to be shallow. If used too deeply, they will wander, as will the simpler center bits used in hand braces. For accurate drilling, there are bits that guide themselves in the hole with parallel, fluted bodies.

Expanding bits make holes from about 1 in. up to 3 in. in diameter. They are intended to be turned slowly in a hand brace. To a certain extent they have been replaced by the cheaper hole saw, already described.

A *plug cutter*, somewhat like a drill, is always useful to have—for those parts of a boat that have to be joined with countersunk screws (heads below the surface) and covered with a plug. This insures that no metal will project and anything rubbing against the surface will only meet wood. If the part is made of an attractive, varnished wood, the plug can be made less conspicuous if it is cut cross-grained from matching wood, then glued in place with its grain in line with the surrounding grain. The plug cutter has to be used in a fixed drilling machine: either a drill press or a stand for an electric drill. The plugs are broken out of the wood scrap from which they're cut with a narrow chisel, then glued in place. When the glue sets, the plug is planed or sanded flush (Fig. 4-8). Two sizes—⅜ in. and ½ in.—should take care of all your needs, but no matter what the size, the plugs will always be about as deep as they are wide.

At one time professional woodworkers claimed to be able to do all their shaping by cutting; they would never stoop to filing wood, although coarse files and rasps were available. In recent years several tools have appeared with replaceable

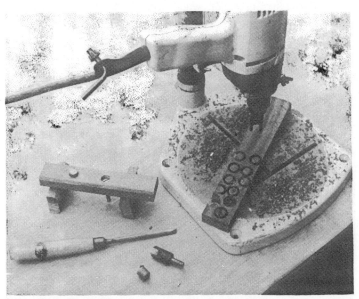

Fig. 4-8. Several cross-grained plugs being made with a plug cutter in an electric drill mounted in a stand. The narrow chisel is used to break them out. The sample piece shows a countersunk screw; beside it, a plugged hole. For appearance the plug can be inserted so that its grain lines up with that around it; when the glue sets, it is planed flush.

rasping blades, that are often professionally employed. They are useful for shaping curves of boat parts, and don't require the skill that is needed to control chisels. These tools, and a supply of flat and curved blades, are really worth having in a repair kit. A flat blade can round the end of an oar handle; a half-round one can trim a hole through a deck for a mast; one with a curve in its length can be used to make a long sweep inside a frame true.

In general, sanding should be regarded as a finishing process rather than as a means of removing a lot of wood. However, a disk sander with a coarse-grit paper can level off a part that has a mixture of end and side grain, without the risk of grain breaking out that there might be with a cutting tool. A belt sander is more expensive , but it's worth the labor it saves on a job such as finishing a planked deck. The finish it leaves on a boat part, like the overlapping plank ends in a transom (cross member), can only be equaled by very strenuous hand work.

The finest finish for wood that is to be varnished is achieved by *scraping*. The edge of a piece of broken glass, the simplest "tool" required, is held at an angle and pushed or pulled over the wood (Fig. 4-9A). The professional tool for the job is a cabinet scraper (Fig. 4-9B), a rectangle of hard steel, held to a slight curve with both thumbs pushing at the center and the fingers pulling back, while the tool is thrust forward. The cutting edge is burred, resembling the wire edge on a sharpened chisel. The burr is made by rubbing the edge against a hard steel tool, such as a chisel (Fig. 4-9C). The burr

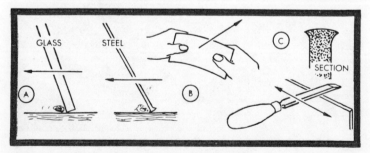

Fig. 4-9. The best finish is achieved by scraping rather than sanding. This can be done with a piece of glass (A), but more professionally with a cabinet scraper (B) held to a curve. The shape of the edge has to be restored often by rubbing it with a hard, flat tool (C).

does not last long, but is easily enough made again. After some time, however, the edge has to be restored to a square cross section by rubbing it on an oilstone. Hook-type scrapers, usually pulled with a replaceable wooden handle, do a similar job. One of these is better for a repair kit than a cabinet scraper; it is also effective for removing the paint around a repair. Sanding tends to bend over some wood fibers that can spring up and mar the finish when varnish is applied. Consequently, scraping should only be followed by light sanding with a fine-grit paper.

The need for a large number of clamps was mentioned in the assembly of a basic repair kit. Besides all the C-clamps that can be amassed, a portable woodworking vise should be considered: clamp heads that can be attached to the edge of a board have uses that are beyond the scope of C-clamps. There may be no justification for buying a new bar clamp, but if one is available cheaply, it will have occasional uses.

Besides the general-purpose hammer of the basic kit, a very light one (about 4 oz) is better for driving the fine brass nails often used with plywood, or for spreading the ends of nails when riveting lapstrake planking. On the other hand, there are likely to be occasions when a really heavy hammer is needed. Along with these, you should pick up any odd iron blocks you can find, to use as anvils, or to hold against nails being bent over (or against nails being riveted); sections of train rails make the most finished looking "junkyard" anvils. If you have cut off nails for riveting, there is no satisfactory substitute for the proper cutters. End (or top) cutters in this application are of more use than diagonal (or side) cutters.

The combination square of the basic kit may be supplemented with a 12 in. square for marking right angles with longer sides. An *adjustable bevel* (angular gage) has more uses in boat work than in other woodworking (Fig. 4-10);

Fig. 4-10. Adjustable bevels are used like combination squares, but can be made to conform to other than right angles.

the angles that have to be transferred for most parts that have to be filled are usually other than right angles. Most convenient is a bevel with a lever or other locking device rather than a screw.

A pair of large, strong woodworking dividers (like a compass without a pencil lead) have their uses for transferring dimensions. The dividers can be used to derive equal spacing between holes along a line, with more precision than a rule or an estimate. (Rivet heads and screws that show in a finished job will look much better if evenly spaced.) An opening can be spanned with the dividers, and then the dividers used to mark its size on the wood that has to fit—without having to refer to a rule.

A stapler is an excellent device for molded veneer construction and repair. The veneers are held with light staples while the glue sets. An office-type stapler can be used to drive them, but if there are many to drive, this method is rather tedious. It is better to employ a spring-operated gun or tacker that shoots the staples in with a squeeze of the handle. The latter is especially appropriate for permanent, nonferrous staples.

Earlier boatbuilders used a number of tools which are becoming obsolete. Some are still around and should not be dismissed as useless if they can be obtained. One old standby worth your consideration is an axe. It is capable of many jobs, and if you can control it, it is certainly the best tool for removing a lot of wood quickly. Another tool common among many woodworkers is a draw knife: two handles at the ends of a blade, used with a pulling action. With its angle set to control the cut, it can take off anything from a fine shaving to a ¼ in. slice. An adze is a relative of the axe (Fig. 4-11). It's effective

Fig. 4-11. Two traditional tools which still have their uses: an adze and a drawknife.

in roughly planing a surface. The older tools require more skill than many more modern tools for the same purposes.

## MAJOR LAPSTRAKE REPAIRS

The method of fastening originally used in lapstrake construction may have to be adopted for repairs, entailing techniques that are different from those used for other boat repair jobs. Although screws may be used in overlapping ¾ in. planking, they are not professionally favored.

In cheaper construction the fastenings are nails clenched (bent over) inside, hence the name *clench construction*. In a workboat, rather than a pleasure craft, galvanized iron nails might be used. For better work, the nails should be copper. In clench construction, nails up to ½ in. longer than the total plank thickness is driven in from outside (Fig. 4-12A), then a piece iron or heavy hammer is held against the head. Inside, the nail point may be merely hammered over—but it is better to first curve the point over a spike (Fig. 4-12B). Then it is hammered diagonally across the grain, burying the point. (If driven with the grain, it may split the wood.)

For better construction, a form of riveting is used which is very effective in drawing the parts together tightly. Copper nails are used; they may be either square or round. The nails are made in many lengths, but all are comparatively thin. Gage numbers indicate the thickness, but in a small boat the thickness is little more than $1/16$ in., whatever length is required. The nails are used with *burrs*, conical copper washers (Fig. 4-12C) with holes slightly smaller than the nail point to be covered.

### Burr Nailing

To use this method, a hole is drilled for the nail first; copper nails can buckle if driven directly into anything except soft wood. The nail should be about ¼ in. longer than the thickness to be penetrated. As it is driven from outside, the head is supported by an iron backing or a heavy hammer. Inside, the burr is driven over the end of the nail with a hollow punch (Fig. 4-12D). If this sort of punch is not available, a piece of wood with a hole in the end can be used, but it will have to be replaced frequently. The burr makes a force fit and will only hold temporarily. The nail is cut off with top or side cutters about $1/16$ in. above the burr (Fig. 4-12E). A light hammer is used to spread the nail over the burr. It is important that the

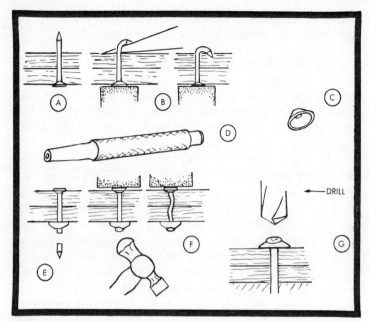

Fig. 4-12. A nail can be driven through from the outside (A) and clenched over a spike on the inside (B). But for harder woods, a burr (C) is forced over the point with a hollow punch (D), the point cut off (E), and the end hammered down—lightly, however, so as not to distort the nail (F). Later, the rivet can be removed with a drill (G).

hammer blows be light; if the blows are heavy, the nail will distort in the cross section of wood (Fig. 4-12F). If this happens, the soft nail may straighten when the boat is used, causing the joint to leak. The hammer may be one with a small ball peen for general use, but for riveting in a restricted area or in a corner (often the case), a cross peen is more useful.

When making a repair, it is often necessary to remove old fasteners. Clenched nails can usually be pried at the turned-in point with a screwdriver, then cut off and driven out with a punch as the head is gripped with pincers. A nail riveted over a burr requires a center punch and a drill. The punch is used to make a dent in the flattened end for the drill, which will break through the rivet (Fig. 4-12). This releases the burr and the remains of the nail can be driven out. It is advisable to drill by hand, as a power drill may go too far. In many cases, another fastener may have to be put through the same hole, so avoid enlarging the hole unnecessarily.

Fig. 4-13. A dory nearing retirement with several patches over its planks.

## Patching

The traditional method of dealing with minor damage to lapstrake planking is to put on a patch (Fig. 4-13). Although this may not seem as craftsmanlike as replacing a section, if it is nicely trimmed, it may be regarded as a characteristic of the type of boat and not a mar to its beauty. New lifeboats were often reinforced with long patches such as these, covering strakes. An advantage of this technique for repairs is that the patch can usually be fitted without removing any existing fasteners.

The patch, a piece of wood, should be long enough to cover the damage by a reasonable amount. It has to bear against the adjoining plank and may be the whole or only part of the width of the plank being covered, depending on the location of the damage. The patch should be made of wood similar to that used in the boat, if possible, and thinner than the planking; but if there is much of a curve it may be advisable to use a more flexible wood or a warped scrap piece that approximates the curve.

Shape the top edge by trial and error to fit against the adjoining plank, then taper off the bottom edge so it curves down gradually to meet the plank below (Fig. 4-14). Traditionally, the patch was bedded down on canvas liberally coated with paint, but it would be better now to use a flexible jointing compound between the wood surfaces and not bother with canvas.

Secure the patch with the same sort of fasteners used in the rest of hull. The spacing between fasteners can be the same as originally used. However, if the patch has to be pulled against much of a curve 3 in. should be about the minimum along the length of the patch. For additional strength, the fastenings may be 1 in. apart in two staggered rows at the ends of the patch.

If the plank to be repaired has a severe curve or twist, it may be difficult or impossible to bend a wooden patch to fit closely. Traditionally, a piece of sheet lead was used in these circumstances. Lead can be easily made to conform to any shape with a mallet. It should be fixed over a layer of jointing compound with fasteners similar to those used with a wooden patch. Of course, lead is rather obvious on wood; this is more of a workboat repair. It is better to clean down to bare wood,

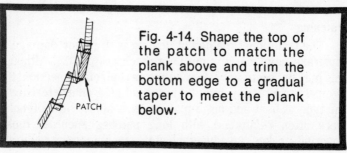

Fig. 4-14. Shape the top of the patch to match the plank above and trim the bottom edge to a gradual taper to meet the plank below.

PATCH

smooth the damage as much as possible, then fill the spaces with pieces of fiberglass and resin followed by fiberglass cloth and resin on the outside. A reasonably inconspicuous repair can be obtained with a final coat of polyurethane varnish.

Of course, the patch will still be visible. In a traditional boat this may be acceptable as one of the signs of its type and history. A patch certainly keeps the water out and usually leaves the repaired part stronger than before it was damaged. The alternative is to replace the section of planking. This is a more involved project, but it is tedious rather than difficult. Some woodworking skill is needed, but a capacity for careful work is more important. The work can be time-consuming, but it is in cost-free time that the amateur scores over the professional.

### Plank Replacement

The procedure of replacing a section of planking is basically the same for a lapstrake, carvel, or strip planking. The work is easier with flush, carvel planking (lengthwise planking wider at the center than at the ends) or strip planking (mainly parallel pieces), because the complication of overlapping edges does not have to be dealt with. The repair methods for lapstrake planking described also apply to the other wood skins mentioned.

The inside of a lapstraked boat is usually braced with ribs made from strips of elm sprung into place. Sawed frames cut out of solid wood to conform to the hull are used with flush-fitting planks in boats that depend on calking for watertightness. Bent ribs in a lapstrake boat may be only 6 in. or so apart, while sawed frames are usually more widely spaced. The location of ribs or frames should be checked before deciding how much of a damaged plank to cut out. If the new piece has to curve very much it at least should be long enough to cover two frames; the technique and work involved is little different than that for fitting a short piece.

Usually joints are made midway between frames. There are two ways of doing this. The professional makes a scarfed joint using an 8° angle, as mentioned earlier (Fig. 4-15A). A skilled worker might scarf the joint without a backing piece between ribs, but the amateur is better off using one (Fig. 4-15B). An alternative is to merely butt the ends together over a backing piece (Fig. 4-15C). The knack in getting a close butt

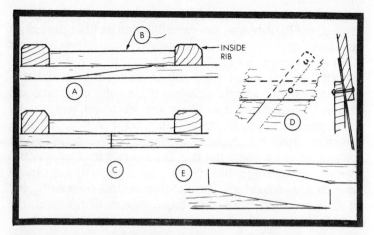

Fig. 4-15. The joint between old planks and new sections can be scarfed (A) against a backing piece (B), or merely butted together (C). Fasteners that can't be punched out or unscrewed will have to be sawed in half between planks (D) before the damaged section can be removed. A scarfed joint will be tighter if the beveled ends are slightly hollow (E).

joint is to make the new piece very slightly longer than necessary so it can be sprung into place.

Mark off the amount of damaged plank to be removed. Remove all fasteners by drilling through burrs inside and punching out rivets, or by cutting off clenched nails. Screws may be withdrawn easily, providing any plugs can be removed and the slots cleared. Try to remove fasteners with a minimum of damage to the holes. Almost certainly, old boats will have fasteners that will defy removal and must be cut off with a hacksaw blade between the planks (Fig. 4-15D). If the blade is angled into the wood that is to be scrapped, the plank which is to remain will not be damaged. Wood can be cut away with a saber saw. If hand tools have to be used, drill a hole to provide a starting place for a narrow-blade saw.

If the joints are to be scarfed, mark and cut the ends to be tapered with a broad chisel, preferably a thin *paring* chisel. The tricky part is cutting underneath the overhanging plank above, because it will have to be done partly inside and partly outside. To insure a close fit between the thin edges, the bevel can be made slightly hollow (Fig. 4-15E). In most areas of a boat the top edge of a new section will require slight beveling to fit under another plank. With the top edge in position, the curve of the bottom edge can be marked, then the new piece removed and trimmed before it is fixed into position.

If the damaged piece is removed intact, it can be used as a template for a new piece; but it is more likely that you will break it getting it out. If the new piece must have a pronounced twist in it, its shape can be more accurately found by spiling.

For a spiling piece, use any convenient, flexible piece of wood that is slightly longer than needed to fit the job. Its width is not important, nor need it even have parallel sides. Draw a center line on it with others crossing it that are spaced about 6 in. apart—but if there is much curve, make lines closer. Clamp the spiling piece across the opening for the new section (Fig. 4-16A). At each of the cross lines, measure the distance the edge of the new plank is to be from the center line, and write it on the board (Fig. 4-16B). Also, mark where the ends are to be cut, and their angle. Remove the spiling piece and put it on the wood for the new plank. At each mark on the spiling piece, measure the distances noted out onto the new wood; then bend a strip of wood through these points and draw the edge to be cut (Fig. 4-16C). If there is much of a twist, this curve is likely to be very different from anything you may have ever estimated before.

The butted or scarfed joints of the replacement piece of planking should be glued as well as held by fasteners to the

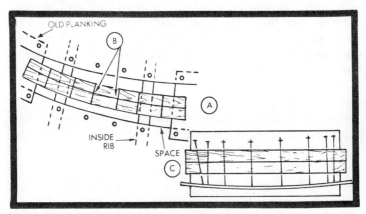

Fig. 4-16. If a curved or twisted section of planking is to be replaced, a spiling piece is made and clamped across the open space (A). Measurements are taken at the marks (B) and transferred to the board to be cut (C).

backing piece. Joints to the planks above and below may be made using fasteners through existing holes. A layer of a flexible jointing compound could be used, as long as it is very thin. A thick layer of glue that sets hard and rigid should be avoided, as it would be incompatible with the rest of the boat, making a hard spot in a hull that is otherwise slightly flexible. Any thickness in the joint could cause a leak when the wood swells after the boat is launched.

**Replacing Ribs and Frames**

The bent frames or ribs inside a lapstrake hull may have been steamed and bent to shape during construction. Eventually, however, they may crack or break completely, particularly in a lightly built open hull that flexes with the motion of waves. An occasional crack or break is not serious, but if there are several in adjacent frames, repairs are called for.

The neatest method, in this case, is to replace a bent frame completely. This is not difficult if it is easily accessible, without decks or other obstructions above. If there are bottom supports or other pieces inside the frame, they can be replaced later. Many lapstrake boats have *risers*[1] on each side that support *thwarts*[2] and other parts. It may be necessary to remove their fasteners in adjoining ribs so they can be bent and taken out to allow the removal of the old rib.

Prepare a new strip for the rib from rock elm or other flexible wood that is the same thickness as the old piece. A rib near the center of the boat can likely be bent without steaming, particularly if there is still sap in the wood. However, leave it bent to the approximate curve overnight, with the ends bowed toward each other and by a rope held in that position. Or spring it between a bench top and the floor.

If the rib cannot be bent this way, it may be possible to get it to take a sufficient curve by wrapping cloth around it and drenching it with hot water. This may have to be done several times before the wood can be put into place while it is still pliable. The alternative is steaming—a process which is not as difficult as it may seem. A few ribs can be placed in a piece of pipe large enough to take them, or in a temporary tube made

---

[1] Upright support members like those between stair treads.
[2] A plank lying flat and horizontally across ("athwart") a boat and supported on risers.

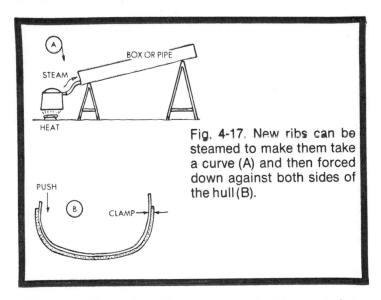

Fig. 4-17. New ribs can be steamed to make them take a curve (A) and then forced down against both sides of the hull (B).

of four boards nailed together. Then the tube is supported at a slight angle, and steam is introduced at the lower end from a large kettle. Cloths are wrapped around the connection of the kettle spout to the tube to prevent leakage (Fig 4-17A). Arrange packing around the timbers to keep them apart, so steam can get all around them. The amount of steaming will depend on the wood and its size, but for a small boat 30 minutes may be enough.

Force the new rib down from both sides of the hull, and clamp to the gunnels when a close fit has been made for most of the length (Fig. 4-17B). Add new fasteners, starting from the center of the boat and working outwards. When enough fasteners have been driven to hold the rib, the excess above the gunnels may be trimmed off; then the remaining fasteners are driven in place. Leave the risers until last.

**Rib Reinforcement**

The alternative to replacing a bent rib is to "double up," or put a reinforcing rib beside it. This is a length of similar wood fastened next to the damage rib and extending over at least two plank laps above and below the point of damage (Fig. 4-18). As existing fasteners do not have to be removed, this is comparatively   a simple task. The only problem may be getting the reinforcing piece the right shape and holding it there while fasteners are driven in. It may be possible to

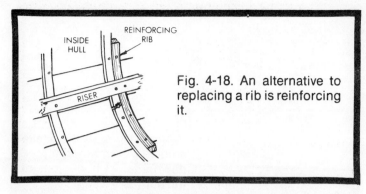

INSIDE HULL

REINFORCING RIB

RISER

Fig. 4-18. An alternative to replacing a rib is reinforcing it.

prebend a piece longer than is needed to more of a curve than is needed, then cut it to size and fasten it down before it loses its curve.

A reinforcing rib would have to be too massive for the broken rib in, say, a yacht with flush-fitting planks; the solution here would be to laminate with three or more easily bent pieces to make up the thickness required. For most purposes, ⅜ or ½ in. wood will take any reasonable curve required. Two methods are possible.

The reinforcing rib can be made as a unit away from the boat. By spiling, obtain the curve of the planking (Fig. 4-19A). Make a *former* by drawing a curve (derived by spiling) on a strong scrap of wood. Draw the curve so that there is an allowance for the total thickness of laminations (Fig. 4-19B). The pieces for the rib are glued together and clamped down with the former (Fig. 4-19C). When the glue is hard, clean off the laminated reinforcing rib and fit it beside the broken rib.

The reinforcing rib can be built up in place, particularly where the planking is thick. One lamination is bent and glued to the skin, and bolts are used as clamps (Fig. 4-19D). When this glue has set, the bolts are withdrawn and another lamination is added and bolted in place (Fig. 4-19E). This is continued until enough laminations are built up. It should then be possible to remove the bolts completely and replace them with glued wood plugs; but if the strength of bolts is considered desirable, they should be made of a seawater-resistant alloy, and their heads should be countersunk sufficiently to allow space for wood plugs.

With these comparatively massive ribs, screws or bolts may be driven through both the reinforcing rib and the broken one for additional strength. Much depends on accessibility.

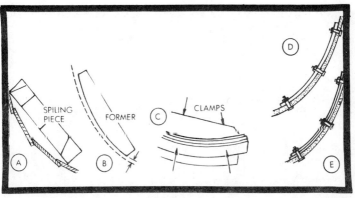

Fig. 4-19. The reinforcing rib could be made in the workshop. The curve of the hull is obtained by splicing (A) and transferred to a piece for a former (B), which is clamped against the laminations (C). The laminations can be glued to the boat and held with bolts (D). The bolts are removed and reinserted for each successive layer (E).

## MAJOR FLUSH-PLANK REPAIRS

Although lapstrake planking has dry joints, flush-planked boats do not, and have to be repaired accordingly. The planks are glued at the edges and, if the planks are narrow, will be screwed edge-to-edge as well. This sort of construction cannot be done during a repair unless the work involves a replacement near a gunnel or similar edge. It also means that cutting out a damaged area will entail cutting through many screws and carefully trimming along glue lines. Replacement planks will have to be thoroughly bedded in glue as well as screwed to ribs, and to backing pieces at end joints. If joints do not meet well, use sawdust and epoxy or waterproof glue to make a putty for filling spaces.

Traditional flush or *carvel* planking is treated differently. The plank edges butt together on the inside edges, but the joint is notched with a *V* on the outside so that the meeting edges are beveled toward each other; then the joint is filled with cotton and calked. Nowadays, calking in the form of synthetic compounds is becoming prevalent; the old type were never very satisfactory for long periods of stress and exposure. It often hardened and fell out. If you find this sort of compound in a repaired plank section, scrape it out for some distance beyond the repair so the new calking can continue along the

Fig. 4-20. Removing calking from the leaking seams of a fishing boat with a narrow scraper.

seam (Fig. 4-20). It may be necessary to make a scraper by bending the tang of an old file and grinding it to make a reasonable fit in the seam.

The replacement plank should fit between its neighbors as best you can make it. If any gaps go right through the seam, force it closed before using any calking; otherwise the cotton strands would go right through. In this case, glue in a sliver of wood from the inside and trim it flush before calking.

### Calking

Calking cotton can be bought in loose skeins. To use it, take a few strands and twist them loosely into a sort of cord just thick enough to fit into the seam (Fig. 4-21). The tool used for this operation is a *calking iron*—a broad blunt chisel. It is struck lightly with a mallet, driving the cotton in. The purpose of the cotton is mainly to economize on sealer. The cotton should obviously be tight, but do not use excessive effort, particularly if the wood is very dry and is expected to swell when the boat is launched. Usually, the cotton should just more than half-fill the *V*-notch.

Calking may be done with one of the elastomeric synthetic rubber sealants, which will not become brittle, yet take paint. Follow the maker's directions. Some sealers, particularly

Fig. 4-21. Loosely twisted cotton strands being driven with a chisel-like calking iron into the seam of a boat.

those with a polysulfide base, require that the seam be primed first to get the best bond. Sealers are pressed in with a putty knife. Work along a seam progressively to avoid air bubbles. Masking tape on each side of the seam will help, but peel it off when the calking becomes tacky, i.e., before it fully sets. Excess sealer can be trimmed off with a sharp chisel.

## Knee Braces

Traditional boatbuilders made much use of *grown knees*, natural wood angle brackets cut from crooks in trees (Fig. 4-22A) so the grain followed the shape. In open boats, they were used at the corners of the transoms and gunnels, at the bow, and between thwarts and any other part needing stiffening. If one has to be replaced, you can use a synthetic glue to laminate something which will probably be stronger than the original. A large number of very thin pieces can be glued and bent around a former (which may be just a piece of pipe), while a small, solid piece of wood is used to brace the laminations at the point of the angle from the backside (Fig. 4-22B). After the glue sets, the new knee is cut from the built-up piece (Fig. 4-22C). The replacement will be superior in

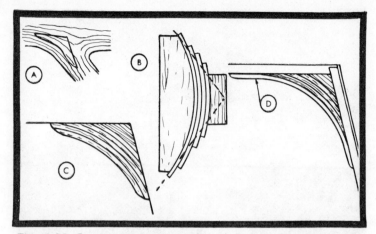

Fig. 4-22. Sections of tree forks, still found in some boats, can be replaced with laminated forms using a former (B); the new piece can be made to conform to the original shape(C) and finished with a decorative, light layer(D).

that much of the grain will follow the curve, reducing the risk of the narrow ends cracking, as they sometimes did in grown knees. An attractive finish can be obtained by making alternating laminations of light and dark wood, or by using a last light wood layer after the knee is fixed in place (Fig. 4-22D).

## MAJOR PLYWOOD-HULL REPAIRS

Plywood hull damage is often confined to a small area only. The cross-grain construction of plywood limits the spread of damage; but because the material is thin, special repair methods have to be used. It would be unwise to leave even a small amount of damage untreated because just one or two broken layers will allow water to seep through the grain by capillary action. At the least, this will cause discoloration under the varnish. However, in cold temperatures, the water in the wood may freeze and expand, causing the wood fibers to break—a condition called *delamination*. Superficial damage may be filled with a paste made by mixing sawdust with epoxy or other waterproof glue. The surfaces must be dry before this is done, most efficiently by wiping with alcohol. If a small plywood area has been penetrated, it can be a regular shape, then plugged from the outside with a solid wood block made with slightly tapered edges held with glue. After the glue sets, the outside is planed off to match the surrounding surface.

An alternative for a slightly larger area is to insert a flush section of plywood plank using a backing piece on the inside. If possible, use a support to hold the backing piece in place while the glue sets. If the boat is small it can be tilted so a weight can be put on the job.

This should be satisfactory for damage to a fairly small, flat panel (Fig. 4-23). If the area is curved, or if it is necessary to cut out more than a few square inches, it is better to use a backing piece shaped like a frame. This way, clamps can be used around the hole to pull the frame to a curve (Fig. 4-24). Later, thin brass or copper nails can be driven through and clenched. The patch is fixed in after the glue on the backing frame sets. In places where the patch will have to conform to a severe curve, a better shape can be obtained by making up the patch with two laminated thicknesses of plywood.

Molded plywood hulls are made from strips of veneer laid in alternate directions, resulting in a stressed skin. Because of the strength of the skin the hull does not need much of an internal structure. In effect, it is a sheet of plywood in the

Fig. 4-23. Before a repair is made in the comparatively flat side of a plywood dinghy, a provisional outline is drawn and checked on the inside by drilling small holes near the damage—to avoid an internal structure or make the best use of it.

Fig. 4-24. A backing piece inside the cutout is pulled against the curve of a hull with clamps; it will be secured with screws and glue. The space will be filled with two pieces of plywood laminated to conform to the proper shape.

shape of a boat. They can be repaired somewhat like sheet plywood hulls, except that molded plywood is preferred for round-bottom hulls. Consequently, there is often more compound curvature to be dealt with in this kind of repair. Usually it will be necessary to cut around the damage to expose undamaged layers of veneer, and fit in new veneers of the same thickness; this way, the repair can be built up like the original construction. The veneers can be held in place while the glue sets with ordinary staples. After they have been removed, wiping the hull several times with a cloth soaked in hot water will cause the wood around the tiny holes to swell and close.

Finding veneers of the same thickness and type as used in the original hull may not be easy. For a small area it may be possible to trim the hole to a regular shape and insert a solid piece of wood. This would require that an overlapping piece be affixed to the inside, if there is not enough thickness to give an adequate area for glue around the hole. The outside of the block should extend a little beyond the outside surface of the hull, so it can be trimmed to match the hull and painted or varnished.

Fiberglass-reinforced plastic offers another way to repair damaged wood. Polyester resin will not bond as well to wood as epoxy resin, so the latter is preferable, although some emergency repairs made with polyester resin have stood up under long use without failing. In a real emergency—when keeping the water out is more important than making a craftsmanlike repair—it is possible to use an epoxy patching compound with chopped fiberglass included; and merely fill the space without attempting to trim the damage in any way. This can be done when the boat is beached and the wood is still damp. If the resin is at least allowed to gel, it may be safe to float the boat before the curing time specified for the resin. The resin setting process is irreversible. Consequently, removing such an emergency repair for replacement may involve cutting out more than would have been necessary in the first place.

Damaged wood is repaired with fiberglass-reinforced plastic using a technique the same as that described for a fiberglass boat. Trim the edges the same way as for fiberglass. Remove as much paint or varnish around the hole as possible by scraping or sanding. A chemical solvent or stripper may clean the surface, but it will dilute any paint in the pores and possibly spread it more, preventing the liquid resin from penetrating and getting a good grip. The repair is then made by one of the methods described for fiberglass. Chopped strand mat is convenient for building up the bulk of the hull, while cloth may be used for thinner layers.

A fiberglass repair to wood does not need to be glossy on the outside, something necessary with a fiberglass hull. Instead, the outside can be sanded to match the shape of the hull. Providing the final sanding leaves a fine matte surface, the repair and the surrounding wood can be painted to an inconspicuous finish. However, make sure that the first coat of paint, at least, is suitable for fiberglass; otherwise, there may be trouble later with paint peeling away. Fortunately, all of the paints suitable for direct application to fiberglass will also work on wood. Not all finishes suitable for wood can be trusted for fiberglass, however, so using the wrong paint could leave you with an unsightly patch after a little use.

Although fiberglass is best suited fo a flush finish on wood, it is possible to build up a shape with it. For instance, if the damage to the skin is accompanied by a broken rubbing strip (protective side molding), fiberglass can be built up over it to result in an integrated repair.

## SHEATHING A WOODEN HULL

The introduction of synthetic resins prompted the idea of sheathing wooden hulls with a waterproof plastic skin. Sometimes it is done to protect a new boat, but more often it is regarded as a method of repair to a leaky wooden hull. The technique can certainly be effective with the right materials in the right circumstances, but it can be materially wasteful and time consuming if the boat is poorly suited to this treatment.

Several methods of sheathing have been tried and several companies supply materials for them. It is advisable to adopt the complete system set up by the supplier rather than shop for materials from different sources, which may not work properly together.

Sheathing will not revitalize a wrecked boat. The sheathing provides little strength and will not hold together worn-out parts. It has been found unsatisfactory to only partially sheath a boat. The sheathing must enclose the whole hull up to the gunnels; sheathing only the underwater part of the hull allows water in behind the sheathing and causes trouble. The sheathing must make a perfect bond to the wood, even after knocks and during the normal movement of a wooden hull. If the sheathing peels away and there are pockets behind it where rot has set in, the unsupported part of the sheathing will not stand up to abrasion and will soon allow seepage. Probably the most important part of sheathing is preparing the wood so the sheathing will adhere.

A new hull which has never been painted or varnished offers the best chance for perfect adhesion. If sheathing is desired, do it at the start, rather than waiting until the hull has seen some use. For a repair, the surface must be as near as possible  like that of a new hull: without a trace of paint, varnish, oil, or other impurities.

If the boat to be treated is old and has many coats of paint, a chemical stripper has to be used. It may also be necessary to use a blowtorch and scraper. Unless you are skilled in its use, a blowtorch is better avoided; charred wood does not make a good base for sheathing resin. Broad surfaces are easily stripped of paint, but angles must also be cleared. On a plywood hull, these may only be at rubbers and keel. On a clinker boat, every overlapping plank presents an angle. Use a scraper to get paint out of all the angles. A power sander may be used where it can't damage adjoining parts. Besides getting all the paint possible off the boat, your aim should be to get even surfaces—although there is no need for the perfection associated with a varnished finish. Scores and scratches have to be filled. If cleaning has left any fasteners standing above the surface they will cause lumps in the sheathing, so they must be punched below the surface or ground flush. What kind of plugging material to use will depend on the sheathing chosen.

At one time, most sheathing was done with polyester resin and fiberglass cloth. This combination cures very rigidly. Unfortunately, most wooden hulls flex, or expand and contract. Something has to give when rigid sheathing is put on a flexible skin: so eventually such sheathing will peel away—at least in parts. Flexible polyester resins are a partial solution to the flexing problem, but after a time, maybe years, these resins lose their flexibility. Although polyester resin seems to make a good bond to a wood surface, tests have shown it to break on impact. Despite all of these snags, there are a great many wooden boats with polyester resin sheathing afloat.

The sheathing should be at least as flexible as the wood. Fiberglass is comparatively inflexible. Some methods of weaving may impart some flexibility, but the material itself does not flex enough to match the probable movements of the wood underneath.

Cloth, used to give flexibility in some kits, include nylon, polypropylene (Vectra) and Dynel. These are used with flexible epoxy resins. The method of covering with these combinations of cloth and resin is less time consuming than using fiberglass and polyester resin, and the result is a much stronger and more durable bond.

Because no cloth will fit closely into sharp corners, they should first be rounded by smoothing in a suitable compound. One method of covering is to smooth the fabric over clean wood so there are no wrinkles. Monel metal staples may be used as permanent fasteners for cloth, and then the sheathing resin may be brushed or rolled on with a throwaway applicator. The fabric will become transparent when fully wetted through to the wood. For the neatest finish, sand the lower strip to a feather edge after its resin has set, then do the same with the overlapping edge later, so successive strips meet flush.

The whole surface is lightly sanded and cleaned before applying the surfacing compound (with a squeegee or other spreader). The object of this is to fill the weave of the cloth. When all of this has set, it is sanded again and painted.

## GLUES AND ADHESIVES

For the thousands of years that man has built boats, he has searched for something that would join the materials and waterproof the joints at the same time. For nearly all of that time he has been unsuccessful. Glues that made strong joints in dry conditions failed when they became damp. Materials that would waterproof a joint lacked sufficient strength to hold the joint unaided. It was not until World War II, and what may be regarded as the plastic revolution, that glues with adequate strength and waterproofing ability became available. They have had a great effect on boatbuilding and boat repair.

Glues used ashore, that use water as a solvent, are strong for their intended application but have no place on a boat. For waterproofing joints, a variety of natural resins and waxes have been used in the past that had certain adhesive qualities, but not enough to be trusted alone. Consequently, the American Indian sewed his birchbark craft as well as putting resin in the joints. The Vikings used wooden pegs between planks while putting moss and clay in the joints to keep water out.

Some of the natural lacs—the resinous insect secretion used in shellac—came near to being successful. Nathaniel Bishop's *The Voyage of the Paper Canoe* describes a trip of 1000 miles from Troy, New York to Cedar Keys, Florida in 1878 that was made in a canoe built of laminated paper and shellac. Although shellac impregnates and holds layers of paper, it does not have the strength to join wood.

There may be occasions when a fastener has to be used with a jointing compound to keep water out, but in most cases today, adhesives can be trusted to make joints that will withstand wet conditions without fasteners. As with many other things, glues are often known only by trade names, the generic name being absent on the package. However, the notes below may help in identifying glues and assessing their suitability for a particular purpose.

Until World War II, the glue that came nearest to being waterproof and sufficiently strong for joining wood was *casein*: a plastic derived from milk. Casein glue is normally supplied as a powder to be mixed with water into a thick paste. When the water evaporates, the joint has reasonable strength and is water-resistant, but it absorbs water and weakens after immersion. Although still regarded as good for some purposes ashore, it has been superseded for work afloat and should not be used for boat repairs. The glues that revolutionized boatbuilding are the synthetic resins first used in wartime aircraft construction. Although there are several different chemical compositions, all of these glues come in two parts—resin and catalyst.

A glue that has had much success in woodworking and cabinetmaking is resorcinol, a very powerful waterproof glue. It has been used extensively in the manufacture of plywood. (The glue line is a reddish-brown color.) Resorcinol has to be used in a very close-fitting joint and kept under an even pressure during the setting time—something approaching 250 lb/sq in. And no part of the joint can be more than 0.005 in. thick—both conditions are unlikely in repair work. Although resorcinol was regarded as the answer to the boatbuilders needs at one time, there are now other synthetic glues more convenient to use and more likely to achieve success; resorcinol will not bond to the resins used with fiberglass.

The most common of the synthetic resins in glues for small boat construction has been *urea*. The resin may be supplied as a syrup, with a shelf life of a few months, or as a powder to be mixed with water, having a dry shelf life of up to 2 years. In one form, the catalyst is a mild acid supplied as a liquid. The syrup can be applied to one surface and the catalyst to the other. When the parts are brought together, a chemical reaction drives out the moisture. The catalyst may be mixed with the syrup before use, but in that case, the mixture has to be used within a specified time, usually about 20 minutes (depending on temperature). In another form, both catalyst and resin are combined in one powder. The advantage to this form is that only enough has to be mixed as needed. Whatever form the glue takes, the setting time will be dependent on temperature; usually a minimum is specified, below which the glue will not set. Most are designed to work at normal workshop temperatures. Increasing the temperature speeds setting. This property can be used in repairs by applying heat to a joint to speed an urgent job.

Urea glue is comparatively cheap and quite successful for small craft which are kept out of the water most of the time. After prolonged immersion, it can weaken.

However, the glue most generally suitable for boat repairs is epoxy. It costs more than the others and for extensive work might be regarded as prohibitively expensive, but its advantages usually justify its cost, particularly in the small quantities usually needed for a repair. The glue not only joins wood, but bonds to fiberglass and such unlikely materials as steel and brass. Epoxy requires no more clamping than is necessary to keep the glued parts touching. Joints can be far from perfect and still be sound. If gaps are comparatively wide, a thickening powder can be mixed with the glue to reinforce it. Perhaps of greater value under repair conditions, epoxy can be used in temperatures well below those unacceptable for other glues—even close to freezing. Epoxy can give reasonable results with damp wood, a special advantage when dealing with an emergency repair.

Thorough mixing of the two parts of epoxy glue is important. Stirring with a stick is best; power stirrers may mix in air bubbles, which would take some time to disperse and weaken the joint. For most jobs spreading should be done with the broad end of a stick; epoxy-coated brushes are impossible to clean. Most makes of epoxy have indicated that they are epoxy by their trade names such Polypoxy. This type turns green when the two parts are thoroughly mixed and ready to apply: a useful indicator. Another is Araldite. When buying epoxy, be careful to see that what you get is only intended for gluing. Some brands are also patching compounds, calking compounds, and putties; all are based on epoxy and are excellent for their purposes, but not as glues.

The plastics industry produces a great variety of glues and adhesives. But some lack qualities needed afloat; for instance, polyvinyl glues, described as waterproof or water-resistant, have insufficient strength for most boat parts. If laminated plastic is used in the galley or enclosed areas elsewhere, however, contact adhesive for similar purposes ashore is quite satisfactory. But it would not do for anything else except decorative work. Some of these, in the form of foams, can also be used for buoyancy. If a glue is described as being suitable for paper, cloth, and wood, its strength as a wood glue would be insufficient for a boat.

## PAINTING WOODEN BOATS

Nearly all wood used in boats is either painted or varnished. Teak may be oiled, and sometimes decks of other woods are left bare and kept scrubbed. The need for subsequent painting should be kept in mind while repairing. This is even more important in matching a varnish finish. Paint—or varnish, for that matter—has to be carefully removed from the damaged area (Fig. 4-25). Cuts from a scraper, or scratches from a disk sander, may be difficult to disguise when it comes time to do the painting; so keep the whole job in mind, including the painting, before you start. As varnish will make blemishes and plugs show, don't be hasty cleaning off a repair that may be impossible to put right later.

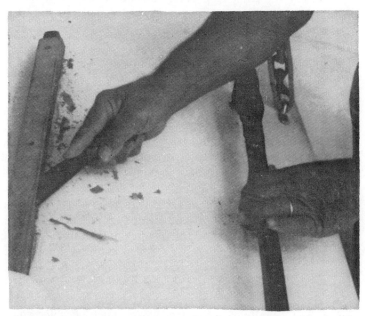

Fig. 4-25. Varnish which has been exposed to hot, salty conditions may flake away, making removal with a flat scraper easy. More stubborn varnish may require a hook scraper or a liquid paint stripper.

Finishing the work around a damaged area of a wooden boat takes more work than it does on some other materials. Where one or two top coats might suffice to inconspicuously cover a repair to metal or fiberglass, the same treatment applied to a wooden boat will not do; the first one or two coats of paint on wood will soak into the pores. The quality and appearance of paint depends very much on the state of the wood it's applied to. New wood should be thoroughly sanded. Open holes above nails or screws should be filled with a compound known to be acceptable to the paint you want to use. For ordinary paint, most are suitable, but for some synthetic finishes, the maker's recommendations should be followed. Give the compound time to set, then level it with the wood. A hook scraper (with a slight curve) is useful for working on a comparatively small area of repair. It should be followed with sanding. The existing paintwork should be tapered around the newly bare wood. A sudden step at an edge of old paint will become very obvious when the new paint is applied.

Ideally the paint on a repair should be the same as the original, and applied in the same number of coats. In any case, the new paint has to be built up to the level of the old, even if the whole surface is to be repainted later.

Along with the new synthetic paints have come new ideas about painting methods. Fortunately, paint manufacturers offer plenty of information in brochures that is well worth studying. Vital information is usually on the can, and ignoring it could result in expensive waste and a far from satisfactory job. If a boat has not had its paint cleaned off for many years, it is likely to have been treated in what is now regarded as the "traditional" way. There is little point in using new types of paint when repairing these, as the difference in appearance between the old and new paint is likely to be obvious.

The new wood can be treated with preservative, preferably one supplied by the paint manufacturer, as some are unsuitable for painting over. Allow it to dry for several days. Plywood is more open-grained than ordinary wood, and some manufacturers advise a special sealer for it.

The traditional method of painting uses a fairly thin layer of primer, usually of one or two coats, much of which soaks into the wood. Its purpose is to provide a good bond between coats of paint and the wood. The primer may not need rubbing down, but if there is any unevenness, use waterproof (wet-and-dry) abrasive paper. This is followed by an undercoat of the type specified to match the top coat, also rubbed down. It will dry to a matte surface, ready to take the top coat, a glossy finish. With some paints, the undercoat can be avoided by using two top coats. When this is done, the first coat must be rubbed down well to remove most of its gloss.

If good varnish has to be matched, the final sanding should be done *immediately* before applying the first coat. Some workers favor steel wool instead of abrasive paper, particularly on awkwardly shaped parts, but there is always the risk that tiny particles of steel will remain in the wood and eventually show as rust. The alternative is bronze wool, available from marine suppliers. Thorough removal of dust is also very important. Varnish does not have as much body as paint, so more coats are required.

Varnish is its own primer and undercoat, but some makers advise thinning the first coat for better penetration of the grain. Each coat should be rubbed down with a medium grit paper and the dust removed before applying the next coat. The quality of the last coat is very dependent on the thoroughness of each intermediate, rubbing-down stage. At least three coats of varnish are needed for a reasonable finish, and up to six may be needed to be level with the existing finish.

## MASTS AND SPARS

Fortunately, most repairs to the wooden parts of sailing gear are of a minor nature and only involve rounding a new part or reinforcing and building up an existing one. Extensive damage is best dealt with by replacing parts. It's usually less trouble to make another mast or boom than to attempt a major repair to a damaged one. Spruce and other soft woods used because of their lightness tend to wear at any point where rubbing takes place. Keeping these places well varnished will do much to reduce wear, as the varnish hardens the surface of the wood, the resin film being harder than the wood itself. Often, however, other measures have to be taken.

The shrouds (mast support ropes) may be fitted with eyelets around the top of the mast and pulled down on chocks (mooring pieces) below. The load presses the steel wire into the wood. If a replacement is needed, make it inset so the wire pulls on the hardwood chock instead of the soft wood of the mast (Fig. 4-26A). Another place that encounters wear is

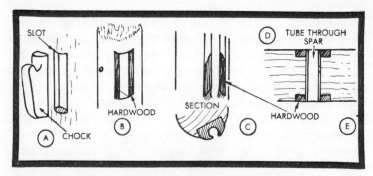

Fig. 4-26. Hardwood chocks should be inset, so ropes rub against them rather than the mast (A). Mounting slots for sheaves should be reinforced with hardwood (B); slots for ropes can be given the same treatment (C). Bolt holes in soft masts can be lined with tubes (D) and further strengthened with hardwood (E).

alongside a sheave (pulley) installed in a slot cut in the mast. In large boats this slot should be lined with metal. If the original sheave is in an unlined slot, wear at the sides may cause a halyard (pulley rope) to jump off the sheave. This can be prevented by putting in hardwood pieces (Fig. 4-26B). This technique has applications elsewhere. If the mainsail boltrope (a reinforcing rope stitched to the edge) has to be fed into a slot in the mast, hardwood side pieces can be used to strengthen the end of the slot (Fig. 4-26C).

The soft grain of a spruce spar will not offer much resistance to compression and sometimes a bolt tightened against it will still not be secure, no matter how much the wood compresses. The solution here is to bore out the hole to accommodate a tube (Fig. 4-26D). The tube may either be of a saltwater-resistant alloy or plastic for lighter applications. If the wood is badly damaged, it can be reinforced on all sides with hardwood pieces glued in and trimmed off after the glue sets (Fig. 4-26E).

## DECK REPAIRS

Repairs to decks and cabin tops are typically minor operations and can be dealt with using the methods already described. If a planked deck is desired instead of an all-over plywood one, the risk of leakage has to be accepted and dealt with. Deck leaks are a frequent cause of rot, so maintaining a watertight deck is particularly important. The days of making special calking mixtures and using them with something of a ritual have passed. Modern calking compounds never completely harden, making a confrontation with a deck leak much simpler, and more positive in its outcome. A tube of a suitable compound should be carried to use on leaks when they occur.

If a leak occurs in a planked deck, try to trace its origin from the inside where the water comes in. Quite often the point of entry will be far from where the drip occurs, due to the water running under the deck and along the ribs. It will be necessary to scrape out quite a bit of calking to provide a worthwhile space for new calking. Attempting to stop a small hole is not usually effective with the comparatively thick compounds available. The scraping can be done with a small hooked tool; it can be a screwdriver, but a scraper made by bending and grinding the tang of a file is better (Fig. 4-27A). Dry the groove by wiping it with alcohol, and press the compound in by hand or with a putty knife. Wetting the finger or knife will prevent sticking.

Leaks often occur around the gunnels of boats. Installing a *toe rail* over the joint will help to seal it (Fig. 4-27B). With a plywood hull, it is important to prevent water from entering here and getting into the end grain of the sides where it may cause rot, or expand in freezing conditions and break wood fibers.

Many small wooden boats leak where the deck meets the cabin, and around the sides of coamings (raised frames around hatchways). Treatment here can be the addition of a quarter section of round molding with its apex that is to fit the corner planed off to allow space for jointing compound (Fig. 4-27C). The back of the molding should also be planed to fit other slopes in the deck or cabin side.

Laying a deck with calked planks requires skill, even in new work. Repairing or altering such a deck may be very difficult because of all the other parts fitted to it. Sometimes the old decking in a neglected boat is so leaky that it cannot be restored to its original condition. One treatment is to cover it with canvas. Another method of alteration is to use the watertightness of plywood and the appearance of planking: The main part of the deck structure is plywood, but thin planks are glued over it with gaps at the edges to take calking and give the right appearance (Fig. 4-27D). The easiest way to do

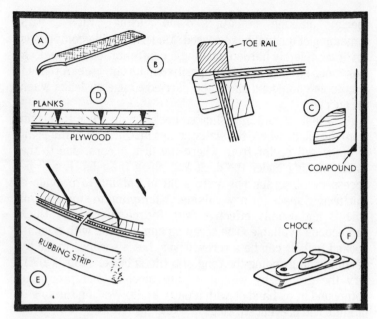

Fig. 4-27. The most convenient tool for scraping out calking is a file with a bent and sharpened tang (A). Gunnel leaks can be prevented with a toe rail (B), and those around coamings with a section of molding (C). A good, watertight deck can be made by laying planks over plywood (D) protected at the edges with a rubbing strip (E). Ropes will not chafe the wood around chocks if they are raised (F).

this is to fit planks all the way to the edges of the hull and cover them with a protective strip of molding: a *rubbing strip* (Fig. 4-27E).

If alterations to decking or a cabin top involve fitting crosswise beams, remember that one of the purposes of the deck and cabin structure is to hold the hull's shape. Strength is provided by dovetailing the ends of beams. This makes a positive lock in the joints, which will resist deck movement in a seaway and reduce the risk of leaks developing.

Ropes and chains passing through bow chocks can chafe the surrounding woodwork. Much can be done to prevent this by raising each chock on a block of wood (Fig. 4-27F). Aim to build the deck, and all that goes with it, into a homogeneous mass. Eliminate cracks and gaps by bedding fittings in jointing compound, gluing down all wood, and coating screws and bolts with jointing compound.

Fig. 4-28. Rainwater leaked through the edges of the deck and rotted the upper plank, which has been removed for replacement.

## ROT AND DECAY

Fungal decay in wooden boats is a serious condition, involving extensive cutting and replacement, or the writing off of the boat altogether. The cause of most rot is moisture with lack of ventilation; consequently, the prudent boat owner insures adequate ventilation to all parts. Saltwater acts as a mild fungicide, so rot is less likely in the presence of saltwater trapped in lockers or bilges. Fungal attack is unlikely above deck level, where ventilation causes swift drying. The waterlogged conditions in the bottom of the bilges restrict oxygen; decay is unlikely there.

Decay is most common just below deck level (Fig. 4-28). Deck stresses may cause slight leaks of rainwater at seams, bolt holes, and under fittings. Closed compartments, such as lockers and the area below bunks may be affected, particularly if damp things are stored there. Of course, the use of nondurable wood encourages rot. Painting may limit water penetration, but a small fault in the paint film will admit water to the wood; at the same time the paint restricts evaporation of the trapped moisture (Fig. 4-29). Even wood on the deck, such as a toe rail, may suffer rot due to moisture trapped under paint.

Fig. 4-29. A rubbing strip just above the waterline has broken away and exposed a bad case of rot, probably because fresh water was trapped behind the paint.

Most types of rot penetrate the whole wood, but there is a *soft* rot sometimes found on very damp wood. This may affect the condition of the surface, but does not go deep enough to be serious structurally. If this sort of rot is identified, it can be cleaned off and the wood treated with a preservative. Unfortunately, rot usually sets in much more seriously.

There are compositions which can impregnate rotted wood. These are synthetic resins which harden in the grain and kill the fungus as well as replace the missing strength of the wood. Successful results have been reported, but there is obviously a limit to the amount of rehabilitation rotted wood can undergo.

The usual treatment has to be much more drastic. Any fungus remaining in the wood is likely to spread. Because of this, it is best to remove all wood that has been attacked—and *burn* it. To do the job properly, go about 18 in. into the apparently unaffected wood along the grain, and 3 in. or so across the grain. This could result in the need to cut away a considerable part of the boat if rot is to be eradicated, and the job could be of such magnitude that it would be beyond the scope of many amateurs. Much depends on the location of the rot; but in any case, there will have to be much rebuilding and replacing of parts.

All replacement parts should be well seasoned and durable. These and the surrounding area should be thoroughly treated with a preservative. Besides replacing parts, the cause of rot should be traced if a recurrence is to be avoided.

Often, complete removal of all the wood affected by fungus is impossible without destroying the boat. Anything seriously affected must be removed and burned; but parts which are still structurally sound may have to remain. In this case, a preservative must be soaked into the grain of the remaining wood. Painting will be of little use. Small holes may be drilled so the preservative can be injected. Using this method, absorption into end grain can be considerable. A hole cut across the grain can be injected repeatedly to allow the preservative to gradually creep along for several feet from the hole. When putting in new parts, all joints, bolt holes, and meeting surfaces should be treated with a preservative, after shaping and before fitting. Some preservatives have an adverse effect on glue, and not all will take paint. The really important thing is to use enough preservative to really penetrate. If a part is small enough, soak it in preservative.

## CHOOSING LUMBER

It is important to know something of the choice and characteristics of different woods, if only to avoid spending too much time on a repair with a wood which rots or splits soon after fitting. Although native woods are readily available, the boatbuilding trade uses a large number of imported woods because of their special properties. In recent years the lumber supply situation has become difficult because of the great demand for wood. Consequently, some woods—mostly with strange names—are being used in place of some of the better known popular types for specific parts of boats. The following should help in assessing the value of a wood when alternatives are offered.

Trees grow with the addition of *annual rings*: each year a new layer of wood is formed around the layer from the previous year. The wood near the center, the oldest, is generally the strongest and most durable when cut into boards. In some trees the outer sapwood (Fig. 4-30A) is of such poor quality that it has to be discarded. After a board is cut, any shrinking will be in the direction of the rings. This can cause a board with diagonal rings to go out of square (Fig. 4-30B), while one that has rings curing from a long edge may bow (Fig. 4-30C). One with rings perpendicular to its length will be the most stable; any shrinkage will be across its length

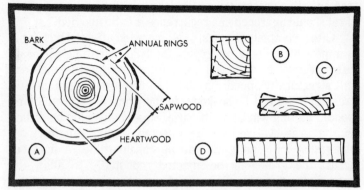

Fig. 4-30. Choosing the most stable lumber for nonwarping properties. A board that has annual rings (A) running diagonally, will warp out-of-square (B); rings curving in from a long edge cause bowing (C). Rings perpedicular to the long side produce the least warpage (D).

(Fig. 4-30D). Timber cut into boards is seasoned (allowed to dry out), either naturally or artificially; ideally this should result in a moisture content of about 10%—desirable for most boat repairs. If the wood to be used has been stored in a hot place and is excessively dry, it will be difficult to bend and may crack. Also, it will take up moisture after fitting, causing problems as it expands.

Wood is classed as softwood if it comes from coniferous (cone-bearing) trees; hardwood comes from broadleafed trees. In general, the names actually indicate hardness or softness, but there are a few softwoods that are harder than some hardwoods—an outcome of trying to keep scientific classifications straight. Most softwoods are much lighter than hardwoods. Knots are more often found in softwoods; providing they are not "dead," that is, black around the edges, they are acceptable, although they should be excluded around points of great stress.

Softwoods are used for spars, work above water, and often internally for cheapness and lightness. It is unusual—although not unknown—for planking to be softwood. It is usual to employ hardwoods throughout, except for spars and places where lightness is important. The following list is not extensive, but it will serve as a guide for the comparison of woods and an indication of where certain woods are likely to be found in a boat:

| SOFTWOODS | DESCRIPTION |
|---|---|
| Cedar, Western red<br>*Thuya plicata* | Reddish brown, straight-grained, light, and with little resin. Used for internal carpentry and canvas-covered decks. |
| Douglas fir<br>*Pseudotsuga taxifolia* | Reddish brown, partially resinous, and of medium hardness. Found in planking, decking, thwarts, and spars. |
| Larch<br>*Larix decidua* | Light orange to reddish brown, easily worked, and resinous. Used in Europe for planking, decking, and beams. |
| Pine, pitch<br>*Pinus* | Reddish brown, very resinous, hard, and straight-grained. Used for decking, planking, keels, stringers, and the masts of workboats. |
| Spruce, sitka<br>*Picea sitchensis* | Light pinkish brown, straight-grained, and free from resin. Used for spars and oars because of lightness, although not very durable. |

| HARDWOODS | DESCRIPTION |
|---|---|
| Agba<br>*Gosweilerodendron balsamiferum* | Light brown African wood used for most parts of a boat as an alternative to mahogany. (Sapwood to be avoided.) |
| Afromosia<br>*Afrormosia.* | A very durable wood that resists teredo worms (shipworms). Has characteristics of teak and is an acceptable alternative to teak. |
| Ash<br>*Fracinus excelsior* | A whitish wood with little durability, but because of its excellent bending properties, used for tillers, boathooks, and bent parts. |
| Elm, rock<br>*Ulmus thomasi* | Pale brown, straight-grained, with little durability, but strong and elastic. Used for bent timbers, rubbing strips, and gunnels. |

| | |
|---|---|
| Cedar (several varieties) | Durable, light, and easily worked. Used for the skins of light craft and general woodworking. |
| Greenheart *Ocotea rodisei* | Very hard and heavy, green, and hard to work. Good resistance to teredo worms. Used in keels and engine supports. |
| Iroko *Cholorophora excelsa* | Durable brownish African wood used as an alternative to teak and mahogany. |
| Mahogany, African *Khaya* | Reddish brown, darkens on exposure. Takes a good finish and is used for most parts of a boat. |
| Mahogany, Honduras *Swietenia macrophylla* | More durable than African mahogany and considered its superior as and alternative for most parts of a boat. |
| Meranti *Shorea* | Dark red. Sometimes used as alternative to mahogany for planking, thwarts, and other parts. |
| Oak (several varieties) | Brown with coarse-textured grain. Found in structural parts. (May stain in contact with ferrous metals.) |
| Sapele (*Entandrophragma cylindricum* | Sometimes mistaken for mahogany and used for similar purposes, but two-way grain sometimes makes working difficult. |
| Teak *Tectona grandis* | One of the best boatbuilding woods, but alternatives may have to be accepted. |
| Utile *Entandrophragma utile* | Characteristics very similar to sapele but more durable—used for similar purposes. |

## PLYWOOD

Modern plywood has considerable value in boatbuilding, but it is important that the correct type is used. Any plywood for boatbuilding or boat repair should be marine grade (it will probably be marked on the sheet). There should be absolutely no doubt about this; anything else is a waste of material and time and could be dangerous. Besides marine plywood, several manufacturers produce *exterior* plywood. This has a similar waterproof glue, but the inner plies may not be of good quality, and there may be gaps between their edges of inner plies. Exterior plywood should be restricted to limited uses inside a boat. Other plywoods, bonded with nonwaterproof glue, would soon delaminate in damp conditions, whatever protection they were given.

Hardwoods used for veneers in making plywood include agba, African mahogany, meranti, sapele, and utile. All of these are durable and have a reddish, mahogany appearance. Exterior plywoods may have any of these outside veneers, but the cores could be of nondurable woods. Douglas fir is also used in marine plywood. It is lighter than the hardwoods, but its coarse grain means more work to achieve a good finish.

# 5

# Metal and Ferroconcrete

A comparatively small number of boats are metal. Aluminum alloys are used for small boats and sometimes for larger ones. Although steel is common in ships, its use for yachts and smaller craft is less common and is limited to the products of boatbuilding specialists: The majority of boatbuilders regard steel as suitable for craft larger than they normally deal with, yet many Dutch shipyards produce excellent steel yachts down to about 25 ft. Other metals are rarely found as main construction materials, but a large variety are used for fittings, equipment, and fasteners.

The word *metal* is applied to the pure or nearly pure extract of an ore; *alloy*, to a mixture of metals, combined to form a material with special qualitites. In a few cases, the alloy additive is not another metal; but the term alloy is generally used. Steel, iron with a small amount of carbon added, is the common example. Aluminum in its pure state is a soft, weak metal. Small amounts of other metals are alloyed with it to give it hardness, strength, saltwater resistance, and other qualities. In the boating world, it is usual to speak of "aluminum" boats when they are actually aluminum *alloy* boats. Unfortunately, there are other terms used in ways which scientists and metallurgists would regard as wrong.

There are a great many stainless steels. Small quantities of chromium and other metals are added to impart resistance to corrosion. Not all stainless steels are resistant to *every* cause of corrosion, however; some are affected by saltwater. In some cases, alloying metals affect steel in other ways. For a long time there was no stainless steel hard enough to be used in tool manfacture.

The most common nonferrous (without iron) alloy is brass, an alloy of copper and zinc. Proportions vary, but around $^2/_3$ and $^1/_3$ zinc is usual to produce the familiar yellow color. Although brass has many applications on a boat, it is far from ideal; saltwater, whether liquid or spray, breaks down the zinc and causes and eventual crumbling of the alloyed part; for instance, brass screws will eventually disintegrate. Bronze, usually copper and tin (or nickel) with small quantities of other metals, is a better alloy. Silicon bronze, a strong, saltwater-resistant alloy, makes good boat parts. In repair work it is advisable to replace brass screws with bronze or stainless steel screws, which were not so available just a few years ago.

Today, iron is only found in cast fittings. Although some cast iron contains impurities, it offers better resistance to corrosion than steel. Wrought iron (worked instead of cast) is little used today, but some older craft have wrought-iron fittings that are still in good condition, demonstrating the metal's resistance to corrosion. Steel corrodes rapidly at first, but the first coat of rust tends to retard further rusting. However, protection is necessary, either with paint or by galvanizing—a method of coating steel with zinc.

Lead has little strength, but is one of the denser metals and does not corrode appreciably. Consequently, it is used where weight is desirable. In repaired boats it is only likely to be found in keels and ballasts. Because of the high cost of lead, cast iron is sometimes substituted for weight, but a great volume is needed to provide the same weight.

Common solder, used for making joints in lightly stressed parts, is an alloy of lead and tin, usually in equal proportions. Spelter, used for brazing or hard-soldering, is a copper/zinc alloy, making it akin to brass. It is used red-hot, but its melting temperature can be lowered by adding silver; then it is silver solder.

A problem afloat is the galvanic action (electric-current production) between dissimilar metals—and alloys—in saltwater. Without going deeply into it, the saltwater and the two metals form, in effect, a battery or more correctly, a cell. In a battery, one of the metals is eaten away as current is produced, while the other remains essentially unaffected. The boat repairer should take note of this and avoid mixing metals, particularly underwater; e.g., nonferrous screws in steel would lead to trouble. Appendix A shows the extent of galvanic action between pairs of submerged metals.

It is close to impossible to avoid using dissimilar metals in proximity to each other around the stern of a motorboat. Fortunately, trouble can be avoided by providing a sacrificial collar or plate near the area; damage to metal in the stern is prevented as the sacrificial plate—usually zinc—is eaten away. In making a repair underwater, the plate may be found in such a state that it needs replacing; if left to be eaten away completely, corrosion of gear in the stern may start. Obviously, it must not be painted.

## TOOLS

The tool kit for metal repairs will largely depend on how much you intend to do. Some repairs can only be done with elaborate and expensive equipment. Their purchase or rental will not be justified for occasional use, particularly if you are uncertain of your ability. For extensive repairs, it would be better and more economical if they were done professionally.

A large, deep-framed hacksaw, with a collection of blades to suit various metals, will be used frequently. A collection of files (12 in. in length) will also prove indispensable. And to hold metal being filed or sawed you will need a heavy vise, solidly fixed to a rigid bench.

Other hand tools should include punches in several sizes, shears, some cold chisels and hammers (mostly with ball peens), and wrenches. If you do much metalwork, you will soon accumulate a collection of hand tools, many of which you will make yourself.

A variable-speed electric drill is essential. For most repair work, a chuck capacity up to ⅜ in. will probably be enough. As some jobs cannot be done by holding the drill, a substantial bench stand is worth having. This may include a vise to hold the work.

If welding is to be done, a disk sander will be needed. For a small amount of work it can be an electric drill attachment; but for extensive repairs, particularly involving steel, a professional-size grinder/sander is needed. (It might be rented.)

A chipping hammer will be most useful for breaking of rust. It has a cutting edge across the hammer at one end and one in line with the handle at the other. It shouldn't be used on plates less than ¼ in. thick, so it is not practical for yacht work.

If much steel plate cutting has to be done, the only satisfactory tool is a cutting torch. Besides cutting steel plate, the torch may be used for other heating purposes. Because the actual handling of a torch can so easily be mastered, purchasing one would be a good idea for a repair not requiring professional help. Many torch "kits" are currently available with throw-away gas canisters, and the cost is typically not much more than a top-quality wrench. But these torches are limited in the usable heat they can deliver, so it would be prudent to assess needs against capability on an individual-case basis.

For other than emergency repairs to a steel boat, welding is best. Welding equipment is probably beyond the scope of most amateur repairers, so if it is considered, its selection and use is best based on the study of a book on welding. For damage needing welding, it is better to make what repairs you can, then let a professional welder finish the job.

Sandblasting equipment, a big help in cleaning off rust and old paint, is in a category similar to welding equipment: it is too costly and involved to justify its purchase for occasional use.

While steel boats are nearly all welded, most aluminum alloy craft are riveted. Small craft are normally made of sheet aluminum thin enough to be cut with shears, so fabricating parts for an aluminum hull takes fairly simple equipment. A *rivet set* is advisable for each size and type of rivet head. This is a sort of punch with a hollow in the end to match the rivet head (Fig. 5-1) to hold it while the other side is being hammered. Then it can be used to mold the hammered end to a more even shape.

For a long time, welding aluminum was considered difficult or impossible. Now, with special welding equipment, satisfactory welds can be made (Fig. 5-2). But the equipment

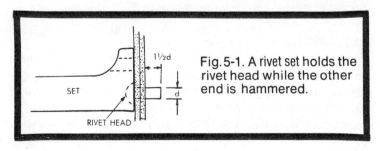

Fig. 5-1. A rivet set holds the rivet head while the other end is hammered.

Fig. 5-2. A hole in the pressed-out rubbing strip on this aluminum boat has been repaired with a built-up weld.

is not for the amateur, because of its cost and complexity, and because of the skill needed. Consequently, any aluminum welding should be done by a professional. When a small amount of heat is needed, as when soldering or brazing small masses of metal (which will not dissipate the heat rapidly), the small gas torches have possibilities.

Some woodworking equipment can be adapted to metals, particularly soft aluminum alloys. Special blades may be obtained to allow table saws, saber saws, and band saws to cut these metals. Belt sanders and other sanders can be fitted with abrasive papers suitable for metals as well.

## REPAIRING STEEL

There are several ways to repair a steel hull in an emergency. The simplest seems too crude to be effective, yet many craft have been saved after a collision with this method: The area around the damage is dried, any flaking paint is removed, it is coated with thick paint, and canvas is pressed into it and painted over. One of the denser types of paint, such as bitumastic or red oxide, would be suitable. The more paint on the canvas, the better the repair will be, but in an emergency or when working between tides, even one coat might be good enough to sail the boat somewhere for a permanent repair.

Anyone who has repaired rusty car bodies with fiberglass and resin knows that the bond between resin and steel is quite good. The same technique can be used for repairing a hole in a steel hull. Raggedness and pitting of the steel can be an advantage. The paint should be removed; excessive rust must be cleaned off—a small amount will not matter. Probably the best source for materials is an auto supply shop. Fitting a patch to a steel hull is basically the same as fitting one to fiberglass or wood. In an emergency, it is advisable to put on overlapping patches of fiberglass cloth outside and inside the damage, besides filling the hole. For a permanent repair, when time can be allowed for it, fill the hole, back it up with an overlapping patch inside, and clean off the outside so the repair will not show through the paint.

Repairs to larger steel craft have often been made with concrete. The same method can be used for smaller boats. Concrete will bond well to *clean* steel, but dirt, grease, paint, and other matter should be removed to leave the steel bare. It would be wise to wipe the bare steel with a rust inhibitor before concrete is applied.

In emergency between tides, it may be necessary to do little more than fill the hole with concrete and roughly mold it to shape, but for a more permanent repair, some preparations and refinements have to be made.

A piece of plywood, or even cardboard, is put over the outside in a way similar to making a fiberglass repair, but the inner surface is first greased to prevent concrete from adhering to it. Some steel reinforcement inside is advisable; how this is arranged depends on the situation. For a small repair, chicken wire held in place with wires attached to nearby parts would work. For a larger repair, stronger wire is strung from rib to rib through holes drilled for it. (Fig. 5-3A).

The concrete inside should extend beyond the hole as far as the ribs, bulkhead, or other structural part; if there is no suitable metal in any direction, a temporary wooden batten may be used (Fig. 5-3B). Although ferroconcrete boats are thin-skinned, the patches should be close to 2 in. thick. A

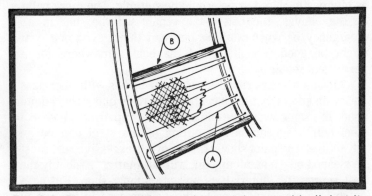

Fig. 5-3. Concrete can be used to patch a steel hull, but it requires steel reinforcement on the inside: in this case, with chicken wire held with wire strung between ribs (A); if the patch can't be made to reach a structural member, battens can be installed (B).

water-repellent cement will give the greatest resistance to water penetration. The setting of concrete can be accelerated in an emergency, but if time allows, proper curing is better. Calcium chloride mixed with cement in a ratio of 1:50 will speed drying, but even baking powder can be used.

For a repair kit, ordinary cement is likely to absorb moisture gradually and become useless, no matter how it is stored. Water-repellent cement will store for a long time and still be usable. A bag of this and some sand is worth carrying, particularly aboard an old steel craft in a doubtful state.

If a professional is to weld on a new section of plating, preparation can reduce his time and cost. All buckled areas should be hammered true, as far as possible. The hole should be squared and the edges should be slightly beveled—as should the edges of the new plate. This way, the plate can be butted against the edges of the hole to form a V-shaped channel around it, which will be filled during the welding process. The hole should be squared and the edges should be slightly beveled. If the new plate can be cut to shape, it should also be given a slight bevel (Fig. 5-4).

Steel decks sometimes suffer before the hull shows signs of serious rusting—usually because of neglect. The nearly horizontal surface tends to collect and retain water, which causes corrosion. It may be possible to patch it in the same way as the hull, but for an overall weakness that could further

Fig. 5-4. A riveted, open aluminum boat. Two bottom rubbers have been covered with sheet aluminum and riveted.

give way, it is wiser to treat what is left with a rust-inhibitor and cover it with a new plywood deck. This can be bolted on, with the bolts going through to strips of wood underneath. It would be unwise to merely bolt to the steel deck if it is in a doubtful condition. The deck and the underside of the plywood should be liberally coated with thick paint just before joining the parts. It may be necessary to trim the plywood decking in a way that will insure that water can run off. Calk any spaces so water cannot find its way between the plywood and the steel underneath.

### REPAIRING ALUMINUM

In a pinch, a hole in an aluminum hull can be plugged with a canvas patch or fiberglass; but for a permanent repair, a patch has to be riveted on (Fig. 5-4). It should not be difficult to get sheet aluminum alloy to match that used in the boat, but rivets are another matter. They will be of slightly different alloy because the alloy used for sheets is not soft enough to be hammered into heads. It is sometimes convenient to bolt a patch on. If this is done, the machine screws will be of a different alloy again; they may be chromed or galvanized steel. In any case, galvanic action in saltwater is unlikely to affect them.

If you don't want the repair to show on the inside, cut away any raggedness and square the opening. It is better to round the corners because there is a risk that a sharp corner may start a crack—the risk is slight, but it is good practice to avoid it. If the repair is merely a patch over a crack, drill holes at the ends of the crack to prevent it from lengthening.

To make a neat repair, use existing rivet positions by drilling out old rivets and putting in new ones that secure the patch as well. The size of a rivet is not always obvious; to avoid drilling a hole too big, drill one that will be cut out with the damage as a check for size. As a rough guide, a manufactured rivet has a head about twice as wide as its shank. Center-punch the head and drill far enough to break it off, then punch out the remains.

The spacing of the rivets in the boat will give you a clue to the best arrangement for those to go through the patch—usually something like four times rivet diameter between rivet centers for an underwater repair.

A snag with drilling in the site of damage is the burr that forms around a hole, preventing the patch from making a close fit. To avoid this, mark the positions for the holes on the patch and drill all holes with the patch removed. Use a countersink (drill bit) very lightly on the underside of each hole to remove any burrs. Put the patch over the hole and mark the position of two holes only—at opposite ends of the patch—and drill them out. Again, remove any burrs. Put the patch in place and attach it temporarily with any convenient bolts, and then drill through all the other rivet holes. Mark the edge of the patch so it will be put back the same way if there is any risk of it becoming inverted when removed. Take off the patch and remove any burrs around the new holes.

Coat the mating surfaces with a jointing compound. This can be a thin coat of a compound used for wood, or a rubber-based plugging adhesive. Some used for aircraft are also suitable.

If there is much of a curve in the area of repair, pull the patch close with a few bolts, then rivet through the remaining holes and remove the bolts as the job progresses.

It is usually inadvisable to use countersunk rivets in thin metal repairs, as too much metal is cut away in making the holes. It is better to have heads similar to those elsewhere on the boat. The plating should be at least ⅛ in. thick for countersinking. To make a reasonable head, the rivet should project about 1½ times its diameter. A good head is easier to make if the end is flat; get rivets of the right length if possible, to avoid cutting the ends after insertion and creating unevenness. Where there is plenty of room to swing a hammer, use a ball peen hammer and lightly tap all around the end of the rivet while the other end is held with a rivet set. The neatest effect is obtained by having the manufactured head outside. Where possible, finish the hammered head by placing a rivet set over it and hammering it tight.

Bolts with countersunk heads will look neatest on the outside if the metal is thick enough to take the drilling; otherwise, use bolts with round heads. Use a washer under the nut inside, and a locking compound to retain the nut. If you have doubts about the risk of galvanic action, coat the bolt with jointing compound.

## REPAIRING SPARS AND FITTINGS

Many spars are made of very light, aluminum alloy sections. The thin metal is difficult to straighten if it becomes buckled. A broken or bent aluminum spar is likely to be incapable of being repaired as good as new. It will have to be replaced. Of course, aluminum is not buoyant, so if these spars are to float, there must not be any holes in them. This is an important consideration for a boat likely to capsize, like a racing dinghy. Any repair must take this into account.

Most spar repairs will consist of replacing damaged fittings with new ones. If rivets are drilled out, the broken ends will fall inside. This may be acceptable, but if not, one of the sealing pieces at the end of the spar will have to be removed so the bits can be tipped out. The sealing pieces will need fresh jointing compound when they are replaced. If the spar material is strong enough to take them, a new fitting may be held with self-tapping screws. Alternatively, pop rivets may be used. If these are a type where the head, shaft, or sleeve falls off inside as the rivet is tightened, the sealing piece at one end of the spar will have to be left off until riveting is completed, so these parts can be shaken out. A pop rivet fixed in place is left with a hole in its center. For watertightness, the hole must be plugged with a piece of hardwood dipped in epoxy resin (Fig. 5-5A). The end can be cleaned off neatly after the glue has set.

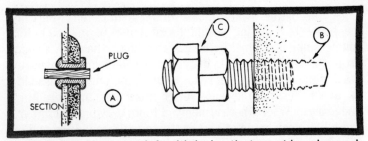

Fig. 5-5. Pop rivets are left with holes that must be plugged for watertightness (A). Studs are made from threaded rod driven into tapped-out holes (B) by turning the top nut of a pair tightened against each other (C).

Sometimes it will be difficult to remove old fasteners in spars, deck fittings, and underwater skin fittings. Bolt cutters may have to be used, but quite often the situation will not allow enough room for their use. A penetrating oil is useful, but it must be given time to work; soaking it in rather than painting it on is the best method. Sometimes, a cup can be built up with putty or modeling clay to hold the oil in place. It may have to be left for several hours before the frozen fastener will loosen. Kerosene may work if a penetrating oil is unavailable.

If a broken fitting has to be built up, or a plate attached to it to strengthen it, and it is possible to drill holes but impossible to use bolts, studs can be used. Threaded rod is used for studs. A *tap* to thread the hole is needed, along with a suitable wrench to turn it. The hole is drilled to the size specified for the particular thread. This should be deeper than actually necessary for the stud to enter, to allow the tap to cut a full thread (Fig. 5-5B). Screw the tap into the hole, remove it, and shake out any metal scraps. The knack in driving a stud tightly is to use two nuts on it (Fig. 5-5C). Tighten them against each other, working with two wrenches, then turn the top nut to drive the stud home. With the two nuts removed, the stud will form a firm attachment.

Worn rudder mounts and similar things are better replaced completely if they are stock types, but if they have been specially made for the boat, they may have to be modified. If the hole in a gudgeon (pivot pin socket) is worn out, it may be possible to bore it out and fit in a sleeve (Fig. 5-6A) if there is still enough metal around it to provide strength. If the pintle (pivot pin) is worn, it may be cut off, drilled out, and replaced with a new piece of rod (Fig. 5-6B).

142

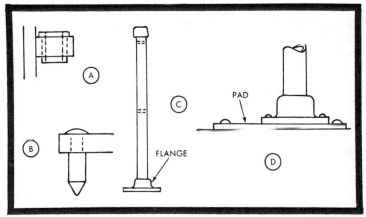

Fig. 5-6. The worn hole in a gudgeon can be lined with a sleeve (A); the matching pintle, if worn, can be replaced with a piece of rod (B). Plumbing pipe and flanges make excellent stanchion replacements (C), and those still in good repair can be improved with wider bases bolted to pads (D).

Deck stanchions (posts) and similar things can often be replaced with built-up parts. Galvanized pipe and flanges intended for plumbing make excellent stanchion replacements (Fig. 5-6C). Many commercially produced stanchions are inadequate in respect to base size. They can be improved by bolting or riveting on larger bases, which are then fastened to larger pads (Fig, 5-6D).

## METAL FINISHING

Steel has to be protected against corrosion. In manufacture, it may be galvanized or plated. These finishes will not prevent rust indefinitely, however, so steel has to be painted. Unprotected steel in a salty atmosphere rusts quite rapidly. In 10 years or so, a ⅛ in. steel plate would rust right through. Rust should be removed from steel to be repainted. A rotary wire brush will do it, or a coarse sanding disk may be useful. Paint stripper can be used to remove particles of paint and to wash off rust dust. This should be done immediately before repainting; otherwise, rusting will start again.

The paint system used may include final coats similar to those used on other materials, but some paints require special primers for adhesion to metal. The traditional paint for big, steel ships is red lead, but it takes a long time to dry, and cannot give the desired finish for yachts. Vinyl paints can be used, but they have to be used with special primers that usually contain phosphoric acid to etch the metal for a better bond between paint and metal. This is followed by several coats of vinyl paint—not necessarily the final color; in fact, using different colors for alternate coats allows an easy check of proper coverage. Ideally, five coats should be applied before the final color is put on. Although this may seem like a lot of painting, the drying time for individual coats is only a few hours; the total drying time will not be excessive.

Two-part epoxy paints can be applied directly to bare steel. They are not as easy to apply as vinyl paints, but dry to the tougher finish. Some manufacturers offer paints which deposit zinc on the steel. Some of these need another special paint above them before the finishing coats are applied. Bituminous paints are often used on steel, but are really more suitable for a top coat of an antifouling finish rather than a decorative one.

In repair work it is advisable to use the same paint system originally applied on the vessel, but when this unknown, one of the systems mentioned can be used. The paint must go on quickly to protect the steel from salt spray.

Aluminum is often left unpainted, but when the boat gets tougher use than just occasional fresh-water fishing trips, it is necessary to protect the outside with paint. The paint will have to be removed, however, in the area of a planned repair. There is often a greasy film on new, rolled aluminum sheet. Detergent and warm water is adequate for its removal. After the surface is rinsed and dried, it may be given a coat of etching primer similar to that used on steel; then vinyl paints can be used. Epoxy paint is a better alternative.

Lead will not corrode, but it is usual to paint a keel on the outside with the same paints used on surrounding parts. If cast-iron ballast blocks are used, they may be coated with a bitumastic paint or the cheaper "black varnish."

Nonferrous fittings are usually left unpainted, but their appearance can be improved by polishing. This is not for surface protection as in polishing wood; and the technique is more reminiscent of wood sanding than finishing: the process involves rubbing down the surface with successively finer abrasives, the scratching of each removing the marks of the previous rubbing. The final scratches are so fine as to be invisible, resulting in polished surface.

Special polishes for boat fittings and car trim may be used; but they are only final polishes. They usually contain something to clean off dirt, but the actual polishing will not produce a shine if the surface is coarsely scratched.

If the surface is scratched, it must first be sanded with a coarse, abrasive paper. This is followed by a finer paper. Steel wool would be useful on intricately shaped parts. A cloth soaked in oil or water and dipped in emery powder or other abrasive will work on those parts also.

The fine abrasive powder should be followed with a metal polish. If the shine is still unsatisfactory, some of the earlier stages will have to be repeated.

A rust inhibitor can be used on the inaccessible parts of a steel boat, but it shouldn't be relied on alone for protection under salty conditions. Proper painting is essential. Similarly, there are lacquers for polished brass and similar metals. These may be satisfactory in the home, but they will not last long afloat. Frequent polishing is the only way to keep the boat smart. When a part is made to replace a fitting, polish it in the workshop before fixing it in place. A power polisher will give a good initial shine that will be easy to maintain later.

## FERROCONCRETE

Ferroconcrete boats have been built for a long time although this material is not common. Only in recent years has the technique of building comparatively thin-skinned boats with steel-reinforced concrete been adopted. Because of its weight, ferroconcrete is seldom used for boats over 30 feet long.

The method of construction results in surprising strength and resistance to damage. Some ferroconcrete boats have survived wrecks, fires, and collision that would have seriously impaired or destroyed craft made of other materials. Any damage needing attention is virtually always only slight.

In the initial stages of construction, the shape is set with a steel frame in the form of rods or tubes. Lengthwise steel rods are attached to the frames, then several layers of wire mesh are attached to the rods. The network of closely fitted wires and rods is then plastered thoroughly with a mortar of cement and sand in a layer less than 1 inch thick. Usually the frames remain in the boat, but sometimes they are removed. In any case, the boat depends on its *monocoque* construction for strength: there are few internal structural members; the skin bears most of the stresses.

The mortar has to be kept moist a fairly long period—perhaps several weeks—during building so it will set to the greatest possible strength. An extensive repair would have to be treated in the same way for the best results, but minor repairs will not have a serious effect on strength if quicker curing is desired.

## TOOLS

Repairs can be made with improvised tools, but ordinary plasterer's equipment works best. Small amounts of mortar can be mixed in a bucket, but greater quantities should be mixed on a board. The casual method of mixing on the ground, allowing dirt and impurities to get mixed in, should be avoided. A small plasterer's trowel is the best tool for getting mortar into holes, although a putty knife can be used for cracks. Mortar can be taken to the job on a *hod*—a square of plywood with a dowling handle attached to its center, carried upright like an umbrella. Surfaces too big to be smoothed level with the trowel are worked with a *wood float*: a rectangular piece of wood with a handle resembling those found on kitchen cabinets.

A straight but flexible strip of wood may be used to scrape the work to get the surface to conform to curves. If several cracks radiating from a point of impact have been filled, this *batten* is across the hull to take off high spots of the repaired but moist area. A brush with very soft bristles may be used later to take out tool marks.

## REPAIRS

Because the close steel pattern occupies almost the whole thickness of the skin and the mortar was cured to give maximum strength, a collision to a ferroconcrete boat will usually only result in a dent; it is unlikely that anything more serious than cracks will occur. Case histories of craft involved in accidents show none with gaping holes.

In some circumstances, it may be necessary to fill a dent to renew external appearance, but whenever possible, a dent should be forced out. How this is done will depend on whether or not strong points inside can be thrust against. A dent in the side may be pushed out with jacks using leverage against engine supports. Spread the force over a wide area with strong boards placed against the dent and the point of support. The job will have to be done in progressive steps, if only one jack is available, to get the approximate shape outside; then localized thrusts may be applied while an observer keeps a check on the work. Looking along the outside towards a light will show up unevenness very plainly. Cracks should be scraped out and all loose concrete chips and dust removed from the damage—with a vacuum cleaner, if possible. The parts to be treated should be moistened before new mortar is troweled in. Only very slight shrinkage will occur as the mortar dries, so the new mortar need only be slightly above the surrounding surface for leveling later.

Various additives have been tried to impart special qualities to the sand-and-cement mortar, built and repaired with the simpler mixture. Beach sand should not be used in the mortar; the salt in it may affect the steel and produce an unsatisfactory mix. Ordinary cement is suitable. If a small quantity of cement is to be carried as part of the repair kit, it should be a water-resistant type that will bond to ordinary cement. Quick-setting cement can be used, but for the same effect, ordinary cement can be speeded in setting with the addition of chloride of lime or calcium chloride. The additive may reduce strength slightly, but in a minor repair the reduction will not be significant. Within reason, the strength of concrete depends on the amount of cement in the mix. The greater the proportion of cement, the greater the strength. For repair work, a mixture of one part cement to two parts sand should be satisfactory. Mix the ingredients dry, adding no more water (fresh) than necessary to obtain a good mix. Thorough mixing with the minimum amount of water will produce the best results.

While jacking out a dent is obviously the best method of repair, if there is nothing to push against, other methods have to be used. If there is room to swing a sledge hammer the material may be safely hit with all the force you are capable of. Even if there is no member inside to push against, it may be possible to work against the opposite side of the hull, using boards to spread the load and a pole to transfer the force of the jack to the dent. However, there will be dents that cannot be restored in this manner. They will have to be filled.

Because a normal concrete mixture will not be strong enough to resist crumbling around the thin edges of a repaired section, it may be preferable to fill a hollow with epoxy and fiberglass. The difference between materials will not be apparent after the job is completed because the hull will have to be painted anyway. Epoxy resins sold as bonding agents for cement mortar could be used, followed by mortar troweled on. If a crack to be filled runs out to a fine, shallow part where an ordinary mix might not retain its form after curing, the epoxy bonding agent should be used.

It is unlikely that a large hole in a ferroconcrete hull will have to be dealt with. But if it is large, a technique similar to that described for repairing steel hulls with concrete can be used. Any reinforcing should be similar to that in the original hull and tied in with it as much as possible. It is advisable to lay on a pattern of wire that extends over the damage inside so a layer of mortar can bond the repaired part to the undamaged inner surface.

New mortar should be left as long as possible to cure; it will be stronger if it does not dry rapidly. The dry period can be prolonged by spraying the repair with water occasionally. Ideally, this period should be stretched out to several weeks during a time when near-freezing temperatures can be avoided. If the water in the mix is allowed to freeze and expand, the repair will be spoiled. It may be impracticable to let a repair cure for weeks, but fortunately, if it is an underwater part, immersion after initial setting will aid curing.

Finally, the repair should be leveled off. Although much can have been done by careful troweling initially, there will almost certainly be the need for grinding or sanding. (A specific grit of abrasive is usually specified for the material to be used.) The hull itself is a material not vastly different from that of many grinders, so abrasives suitable for other materials would be merely rubbed away themselves. Be careful of enthusiastic grinding; the wire reinforcement must not be exposed.

When it comes time to do the necessary painting after the repair has been made, try to use what was used before. The most critical part of the finish is the first coat. Although bitumastic paint can be used, epoxy resin paint makes a better first coat. It will act as a water barrier and bond the particles of sand to the surface. Further coats of epoxy paint can follow, but acrylic paints will work successfully also.

# Working With Fabrics

6

Over the centuries, sails, awnings, and similar things were made from skins and materials woven from all kinds of fibers. In some parts of the world, material better described as *matting* may still be found in sails. Sails of large ships, at the height of their use, were made of cotton, hemp, and flax, often in extremely heavy grades. Techniques used for modern canvas repairs developed from the heyday of sails.

Before synthetic cloths, most pleasure craft had cotton sails. New yachts, almost universally, have Dacron working sails and nylon spinmakers. There is too much stretch in nylon for working sails. For small yachts and dinghies especially, the lighter, less bulking synthetic cloths are better than canvas used for the same purposes. The biggest advantage of synthetic materials is their high resistance to rot. If cotton sails are packed wet for more than a brief period, they will inevitably rot. Mildew, appearing as black spots, is a mild form of rot. It may not affect strength very much, but it can mar a sail's appearance. Preparations can be applied to disguise mildew, but they will not alter its effect. Dacron has a much higher resistance to stretching and distortion than cotton.

Canvas made from natural fibers is often treated with a solution to protect it against water absorption and rot. The treatment tends to stiffen and harden the canvas as well as add to its weight. Because of this, it is unusual to see such material used in small craft sails; but boat covers, screens, and other canvas goods are normally so treated. The weight per square yard of canvas is determined before it is treated. The solution also shrinks canvas, so the quoted width of a piece may be slightly more than it actually is.

Canvas is closely woven of *warp* threads going lengthwise and *weft* threads that go across; the turned-back weft edge is called the *selvedge*. The selvedge can be used without the risk of it unraveling, but any other cut edge will have to be protected. In some canvas a colored thread runs parallel with the selvedge, about an inch from it. This *selvedge stripe* serves as a guide when pieces of canvas are sewn together to make up a wider piece.

"*A stitch in time saves nine*" is a saying that comes from the days of big sailing ships. If slight damage in a sail is neglected, it will easily develop into bigger damage if not promptly attended to. Although such jobs as putting a new panel in a racing sail is best left to a professional with the proper machine, most minor repairs can be done on board by hand. Sails on a small dinghy can be repaired with methods and techniques comparable to those used for dressmaking, but anything larger or heavier will require an effort far beyond that encountered in household needlework.

## TOOLS

Sewing is done with strong synthetic, cotton, or hemp thread. The last two, natural fiber threads, are sometimes found on synthetic sails, but they may rot and give way before the synthetic material wears out; it is usually better to use synthetic thread, preferably waxed. Not only does the wax help the stitches stay put and make for a neat job, it also acts as waterproofing. If the thread is not already waxed, it can be drawn through a ball of beeswax, paraffin, or even a candle stump. The existing thread will give a clue to the thickness to choose for a repair. Extra strong thread is sold as *sail twine*.

Sail needles have a special shape: round at the eye end, but triangular behind the point (Fig. 1-A). The shape creates a hole wide enough for the thick thread to pass through easily. Sail needles are made in many sizes denoted by a gage thickness. The lower numbers indicate very large needles intended for work much coarser than likely to be needed for a boat. For the heavy canvas used for covers and bags, sizes 8 to 14 are suitable. The smaller sizes in half gages from 14 to 18 are suitable for small-yacht and dinghy sails. Needles are cheap, so it is worthwhile building up a large stock. The smaller needles can be protected from rust by pushing them into the bottom of a cork stuck into a bottle. Cases with screw-on tops are available for the same purpose. Another alternative is to push the needles through canvas and roll them up.

Sail needles are pushed through material with a *sailmaker's palm*, a piece of leather with a metal pad that fits over the palm of the hand and has a hole for the thumb (Fig. 6-1B). In use, the point of the needle is held between the first finger and thumb, while the threaded end rests on the metal pad. With the point inserted in the canvas, the whole hand is able to push the needle through (Fig. 6-1C). Sailmakers' palms are mostly made right-handed, but left-handed ones can be found if you are willing to search for them. Professionals also use a *roping palm*, a stronger version for sewing rope to the edge of a sail; but this job can be done with an ordinary palm in repair work.

A good knife and scissors are the only other essential canvasworking tools needed. The professional's *seam rubber*, often elaborately carved, can be dispensed with in favor of an ordinary knife handle. The essential part is the well-rounded flat end used to rub down folds in canvas (Fig. 6-2A).

A *sailmaker's hook* is useful for seams that have to be sewn for more than a few inches. The sharp steel hook has a cord that can be anchored to something firm while seams are pulled taut. One hand pulls against it while the other does the sewing. It is a help if the hook has a swivel (Fig. 6-2B). The expert sews while sitting on a low bench with his work over an apron to protect his thighs.

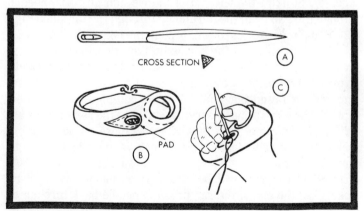

CROSS SECTION

A

C

PAD

B

Fig. 6-1. Sail needles (A) are pushed through material with a sailmaker's palm (B & C).

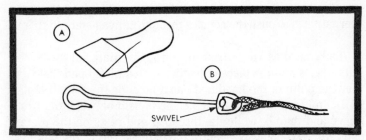

SWIVEL

Fig. 6-2. A seam rubber (A) is used to rub down folds in canvas, as when hems are made. The hem stitching is pulled taut against a sailmaker's hook (B); the hooked end holds the canvas and the other end is anchored with the cord.

Special tools will be required if eyelets, grommets, and fasteners are to be put in a sail, although a certain amount of improvisation is possible. The *marlinespike* and *fid*, both used to separate strands of rope, are also of use to a canvas worker.

## SIMPLE REPAIRS

It is possible for canvas to tear for a short distance. In a sail, stresses may cause the rip to lengthen if nothing is done about it. At sea, an emergency repair may be needed to hold the edges together to prevent air from blowing through. For a short rip this may be all that is needed, but for greater damage, it will later have to be removed and patched.

The stitch used to pull edges together is the *herringbone*. To make this stitch, thread the needle and knot the ends together. Start at the left end of the rip and push the needle through the gap from the top and up through the far side (Fig. 6-2). Bring it across and down through the near side. As you do this, bring the point of the needle up through the rip between the edges to the left of the crossing stitch. Pull the stitch tight, go over the crossing stitch to the right, through the gap, and go through the far edge again. This is the complete action, to be repeated as often as necessary. If you want the repair to be as airtight as possible, get the stitches as close as possible by making alternately long and short ones. Staggering the stitch this way allows the strain to be shared between different threads; the canvas will be stronger, although not as neat looking. At the end of the rip, pass the needle back through a few stitches before cutting off the thread. It will help to rub wax on the stitches and smooth them down with a seam rubber.

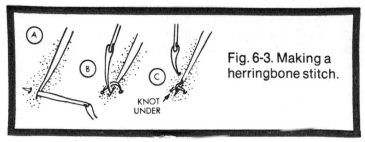

Fig. 6-3. Making a herringbone stitch.

KNOT UNDER

Sometimes rails and ropes are covered with canvas to provide hand grips. The herringbone stitch is ideal for the turned-under edges of canvas in this application, as the tension of the stitches can be regulated to draw the canvas tight. The locking action of the stitch prevents seams from opening too far, so an early repair of only a few stitches can be made by sewing over the worn thread ends to secure them.

Another use of a herringbone stitch is in dealing with canvas torn under tension, such as a rip in the skin of a canoe. In this case, a patch will be stuck on, making it unnecessary to make very close stitches. The spacing will depend on the type of material and the amount of tension, but about ¼ inch is usually adequate. An advantage of the herringbone stitch for this purpose is that it can be worked from one side. If the other side is inaccessible, it will not make any difference.

If there is much tension needed to bring the torn edges together, the crossing of the herringbone stitch will help to lock each stitch as it is made and pulled tight. This crossing, however, tends to make a lump which would show through a patch. If great tension is not needed, the lump can be avoided by using a simple zig-zag stitch (Fig. 6-4A). It can be gone over a second time if necessary (Fig. 6-4B).

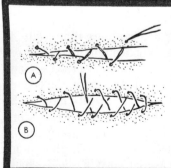

Fig. 6-4. Herringbone stitches create lumps that can be seen beneath patches. This can be avoided in situations where great stitch tension is not necessary by using a zig-zag stitch (A). The stitch can be strengthened by doubling back over it (B).

Any patch stuck on fabric will be more secure if its corners are rounded and the edges frayed. Square-cut corners are more likely to lift and give way. Plastic-coated fabric can be better secured with adhesive waterproof tape put over the stitching. The type with fabric included in the plastic backing is very durable and its use can often be regarded as a permanent repair.

Because the tape will not usually stick very well to woven fabric, a patch for this material should be made of a similar material in a lighter grade. The waterproof adhesive chosen should be one that will penetrate the fabric and be flexible when dry. Most require that both surfaces to be joined be coated and left to get tacky before being brought together under pressure. Usually, the adhesive will grip fast enough to allow a damaged canoe to be put back in the water almost immediately.

The part to be patched should be clean. Oiliness from impurities floating on the water which would interfere with good adhesion can be removed with alcohol or other solvent. Alcohol will also remove water from fabric. If the canvas being repaired is painted, it should be scraped with a knife to remove any gloss and expose the weave of the fabric. Rubberized fabric, used for folding canoes and kayaks, should be patched with a rubber-based adhesive and patch—plastic-based adhesives won't do. Bicycle puncture repair materials may be used.

Latex-based adhesives or cements can be used to fix patches to light woven fabrics. Although they may be used on light canvas, they can be messy and will disfigure sails. In the cabin, however, they are useful for joining carpeting and other materials that have open-weave backings.

## ADVANCED REPAIRS

Most canvas sewing involves nothing more than a simple repetitive stitch, although different applications have different names. The cut edge of a piece of canvas is protected and strengthened by *tabling*—a broad hem. Normally, the edge is merely turned under (Fig. 6-5A), but if eyelets have to be fitted, there is some advantage in turning in enough for a third thickness (Fig. 6-5B). The tabling along a selvedge might be adequate without turning it under (Fig. 6-5C), but more usually it is treated the same way as a cut edge. The folds should

154

be rubbed down hard before stitching to define them and make the stitching neater.

How much thread to put in a needle is a matter of personal preference. For tabling, and nearly all stitching, the thread is used double, and except for a herringbone stitch, the ends are normally unknotted. To start tabling, hold 1½ in. of the thread ends against the folded edge of the hem (Fig. 6-5D) while you push the needle through the back of the material near one end of the hem; sewing the first few over-and-under stitches will secure the thread ends. The usual spacing of stitches is 5 or 6 per inch, but this will depend on the material and the thread. Light sails and fine thread will obviously allow closer stitching, but never as close as machine stitching.

Initially, stitches can be made with the canvas loose, but once they are made, work will progress quicker and more neatly if a sailmaker's hook is used (Fig. 6-5E). If a new length of thread has to be introduced, twist about 1½ in. of the combined ends together along the seam and continue sewing over them (Fig. 6-5F.) Pass the needle back under four or more stitches at the end of the seam (to repeat the arrangement at the start of the seam) and cut off the thread (Fig. 6-5G.) In sewing a tabling, there is a tendency to fold the canvas back on itself as an aid to pushing the needle through

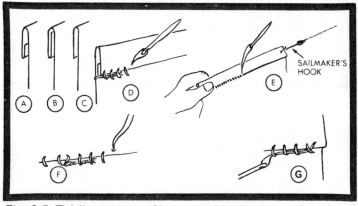

Fig. 6-5. Tabling, a type of hem used on canvas, takes three forms (A, B, & C). The thread ends are secured near the start of the seam with the first few stitches (D), and the work is held taut with a sailmaker's hook (E). Additional thread can be twisted around the ends of that preceding it, and sewn over (F); the work is completed the same way (G).

the combined thicknesses of fabric. This does not matter, but care is needed to get the stitch tension right, not overtight, so the finished job will lay flat.

If two pieces of canvas have to be joined edge-to-edge, they should be overlapped in a flat seam. Selvedges can be laid flat, one on top of the other, as far as the selvedge strip. But cut edges must be turned under and rubbed down. It would help to mark the amount of overlap with chalk. One edge is sewn in the same way described for a tabling, then the job is turned over and the other edge sewn the same way.

A quicker method of joining edges together uses a round seam. This is not very satisfactory, as raw edges are exposed and only one line of stitches takes the strain, but in an emergency it is the most practical method to use. The two edges are folded back about ½ in. and rubbed down. If there is a front and back (as in some treated fabrics) the folds are made towards the back and then brought together (Fig. 6-6A). They are sewn with doubled thread, using stitches spaced about the same as for tabling employed the same way (Fig. 6-6B). A round seam can be sewn quite rapidly if the work is pulled against a hook.

Another use for a round seam is in putting a bottom in a bag. A canvas bag can afford useful practice for bigger jobs. The top edge, a tabling, may have eyelets or a draw string. The long seam along the side is flat, while the bottom takes a round seam. The disk for the bottom should be big enough to be turned in; the bottom is put in with the bag inside out (Fig. 6-6C). Adjustments to the amount of overlap can be made after

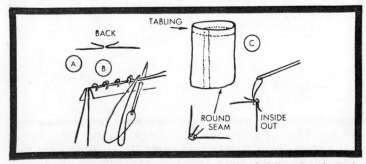

Fig. 6-6. Canvas panels can be joined by folding back their edges (A) and sewing them together back to back (B). Bags (C) take flat seams down the side and round seams around the bottom.

the bottom has been sewn about three-quarters of the way around, so as to finish correctly. The bag is then turned the right way and pushed into shape.

Many yachts have a mast that passes through a hole in the deck, held in place with wedges, and made watertight with a canvas coat (in the shape of a cone). It would be better to replace the traditional canvas with a plastic-coated fabric. If there is no coat to use as a pattern, a template can be made from a piece of paper. Experiment with the shape shown in Fig. 6-7A. The coat will be secured to the deck with a wood or metal ring encircling the mast. If you must use a solid ring, rather than one made from joined halves, it should be put in place before the mast is installed. After the circular piece is sewn into a cone with a flat seam, put it on the mast upside-down, and lash its apex securely to the mast (Fig. 6-7B). Pull the canvas down over the lashing and trap the lower edge under the ring (Fig. 6-7C). Screw the ring to the deck; to prevent water from running underneath, apply a jointing compound under the coat.

Putting on a patch with hand sewing uses an adaption of the flat seam technique. The damaged area is trimmed, as closely as possible, to a rectangle. Cuts are made into the

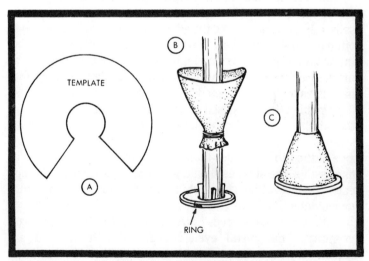

Fig. 6-7. A template is used (A) to lay out the size of a mast coat, similar in appearance and function to a gearshift boot (C); it is lashed to the mast upside-down (B), then turned right-side-out and held to the deck with a ring.

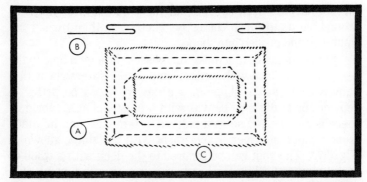

Fig. 6-8. To patch a hole in canvas, trim it to a rectangle, make diagonal cuts in the corners, and fold the edges back (A); then fold the edges back on a patch to match the edges of the hole (B) and sew the pieces together.

corners, and the edges are folded outwards (Fig. 6-8A). The patch is made from the same material, and must be large enough to have its edges turned in for sufficient overlap. An inch or so all around is usually enough (Fig. 6-8B). The patch is sewn all around to the main piece of canvas, with the stitches used for a flat seam (Fig. 6-8C).

Modern sailmakers have found ways to avoid the tedious job of using rope to strengthen their sails; but many heavy sails rely on rope around the edges. Stitching at the roping is often the first to give way in frequently used sails. Because an immediate repair is so simple, it would be foolish to incur the extra labor that inevitably accompanies "pulled" stitches that have been too long neglected.

Doubled thread is used to hold the rope against a tabling; the stitches have to be regulated to suit the size of the rope strands as each is taken up with a stitch. The roping is on one side of the tabling rather than directly under the edge. As far as possible, the stitches should go *around* rather than *through* each strand, although catching rope fibers is sometimes unavoidable.

Many canvas goods have holes strengthened with grommets, but metal eyelets are easier to fit and are satisfactory for most purposes. Reefing points in a sail are normally edged with grommets: little circular three-strand ropes made from a single strand of ordinary rope. To make a grommet, take a piece of three-strand line and untwist it, being careful not to disturb the natural kinks in the rope.

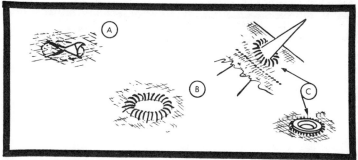

Fig. 6-9. Grommets are installed over the folded points of a crisscross cut in the canvas (A) and sewn down with spiral stitching around the hole (B). For protection against friction, a thimble can be inserted into a grommet widened with a fid (C).

Take out one strand and twist it around itself in three strands so that the kinks mesh with each other. Cut off the surplus ends. For this purpose there is no need to secure the ends (they will be covered by stitching), but if a larger ring is made in this way, it should be tucked (as in splicing ) or sewn over with canvas.

If an old grommet has to be replaced, carefully pick out the old stitches so as not to disturb the cut canvas. The area for a new installation is crisscross cut (Fig. 6-9A). Fold over the resulting canvas flaps and place the grommet on top of them; then stitch the pieces together (Fig. 6-9B). Make a tight bank of close stitches around the inside of the hole, but avoid letting two adjoining stitches pull on the same strand of fabric by varying the lengths of the stitches. Sometimes brass *thimbles* are used to protect grommets from the friction of ropes moving through them. But these can only be used with grommets that were sewn to fabric that was stretched beforehand.

To accept the thimble, the grommet is forced wider with a *fid* or spike (Fig. 6-9C). The thimble is pressed in immediately after the fid is withdrawn, before the hole shrinks back to its original size. If the final tightness is not adequate, the work can be laid on a flat, hard surface and flattened with a hammer.

Brass eyelets used for canvas consist of two parts: eyelet proper, and a ring. Eyelets which merely fold back on themselves without a ring are intended for leather, not canvas.

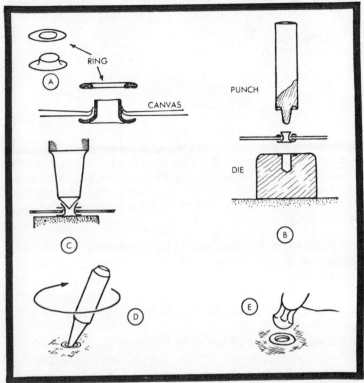

Fig. 6-10. Eyelets are pushed through crisscross cuts in canvas and spread over a ring (A) with a punch and die (B). An alternative is to spread the eyelet (C) and roll the edge with a punch (D), followed by peening (E).

Satisfactory fitting can only be done with the tools intended for the eyelet size used. A punch and die will do a better job than a plier-type tool because eyelets will not grip will unless a great deal of pressure (more than that obtainable using plier leverage) is used to close them completely.

Take a crisscross cut (as you would for a grommet) and push the eyelet through (Fig. 6-10A). Press the ring over the top, trapping the canvas points. Use a punch and die to spread the eyelet over its ring (Fig. 6-10B), and tap it with the flat side of a hammer—but not hard enough to distort the eyelet. If the proper tools are unavailable, spread the eyelet slightly with a center punch (Fig. 6-10C), and then roll it around to spread the eyelet more (Fig. 6-10D). The punch is followed with a ball peen hammer (Fig. 6-10E). The result may not be perfectly symmetrical, but it should be secure enough for an emergency repair. For maximum security, the eyelet should be put through a treble thickness of tabling. The ragged hole left when an eyelet gets pulled out makes it impossible to use a replacement the same size. A larger one would be acceptable, if there is enough canvas left to be trapped between the eyelet and ring.

If the replacement has to be the same size as the original, the canvas will have to be patched to provide a strong place for it. If the repair is to an edge, the patch can be wrapped over it and turned under on one or both sides and sewn to provide more thickness for the eyelet to grip (Fig. 6-11).

Fasteners may grip canvas with a pressing action, a swivel, or a spring, but most are fixed to canvas with tabs that are bent over opposing metal parts; the main part is supported on something solid as the tabs are turned over with a hammer. (Special tools are not needed.) Fasteners attached to solid base parts, such as a cockpit cover fixed to a coaming, will pull away gradually as the canvas shrinks; some slack must be allowed in such areas. Make it a rule to not cut away any more canvas than is needed for any type of fastener. Leaving as much canvas as possible will insure the greatest strength.

### CANVAS DECK REPAIRS

At one time, painted canvas was used to cover the decks of small yachts. The canvas provided waterproofing and a very good nonslip surface. Modern versions for a similar purposes are made of plastic in a variety of patterns. They are either nonslip coated or colored to look like wood planking. These materials resist weather, water, and solvents very well without paint.

A painted canvas deck can only be repaired or replaced when the original method of fitting is understood. The fairly

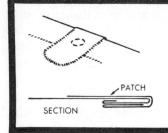

PATCH

SECTION

Fig. 6-11. If a replacement eyelet larger than the original is needed in an edge, the area should be strengthened with a hemmed patch.

Fig. 6-12. Canvas, covering a deck, should terminate in an edge that goes over the gunnel and be held down with molding (A); the turned-up canvas along the side of a cabin can be treated similarly (B); long joints have to be made by tacking down staggered pieces (C) before the seam is made (E).

strong grade of canvas used, usually 12 ounces or more per square yard, is not treated with preservatives or weatherproofing. Treatment would interfere with paint penetration. Canvas sections may be sewn together, but joints will have to be folded over and tacked to the deck, as will patches.

The canvas has to be arranged to shed water. Water must not be allowed to run into openings and get trapped underneath. This can be accomplished at the edge of the deck by running the canvas over the gunnel and topping it with a wood molding (Fig. 6-12A). A quarter-round molding will produce the same effect placed over turned-up canvas along a cabin side (Fig. 6-12B). The canvas should not be cut around deck fittings; the fittings will have to be removed and placed on on a layer of jointing compound after the canvas is put down. Be careful not to cut the fabric any more than necessary when you drill the screw holes. Joints in canvas decking are made by interlocking folded edges and nailing them down with copper tacks (Fig. 6-12C). Short joints can be made by folding and rubbing down the canvas in one operation. Long joints require a two-stage technique.

Long joints are easier to make with selvedges rather than cut edges. Put the lower piece in its final position, and the other upside-down over it, about ½ in. back from its edge (Fig. 6-12D). Drive a line of copper tacks into the edge of the top piece. Use ½ or ¾ in. tacks spaced 3 or 4 in. apart, depending on the stiffness and thickness of the canvas. If the canvas is stiff enough to stay in place, the tacks may be more widely spaced at this stage.

Fold the protruding edge over the top piece (Fig. 6-12E), and rub it down to make a permanent crease for the next stage; if the crease won't hold, use a few tacks. Do not use an adhesive—it will interfere with paint penetration. Turn the top piece over the crease, its final position, and tack down the joint (as in Fig. 6-12C). Tacks, having larger heads, will grip the canvas well, but for appearance, finer copper or bronze nails may be substituted.

The canvas has to be stretched really taut over the deck. "But how, then," you might ask, "can curves be followed?" Allowing slack in the covering won't do; creases not only spoil appearances, they allow water to be trapped. The usual method takes advantage of a triangular framework's inability to be pushed out of shape (no matter how loosely its corners are joined). Using this geometric fact, canvas can be stretched smoothly over any shape. Ignoring paint or adhesive at this stage, the fitting of canvas to a foredeck provides an example for the method. The canvas is first tacked down along a long center line running the length of the deck (Fig. 6-13A). A pull is made at about halfway along the gunnel, in effect extending a triangle whose base is the center line (Fig. 6-13B). Pulling the aft corner creates another triangle (Fig. 6-13C). Further pulls are made midway between two previous ones (Fig. 6-13D). Pull first across the deck and over the gunnel, tacking down the canvas over the edge without relaxing the pull (Fig. 6-13E). Drive a tack into each point of pull, and cover them with molding. Cut off the excess canvas so that the cut edge will not show below the molding. A common fault is to put the edge of the molding level with the edge of the gunnel (Fig. 6-13F), creating a trap for water; put it below the edge (Fig. 6-13G).

If there is a vertical surface, such as a coaming or cabin front immediately against the aft edge of the foredeck, the first pull should be made against that edge towards the gunnel (Fig. 6-13H). Tack the canvas to the gunnel to take the strain, and make the next pull about midway towards the stern (Fig.

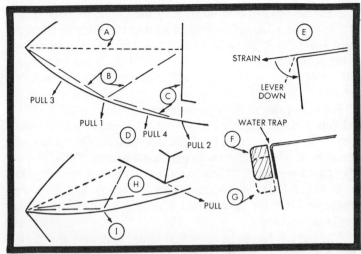

Fig. 6-13. How canvas can be made to follow a curve while being stretched taut over a deck.

6-13I). Better leverage can be obtained in the canvas-tugging operation with upholsterer's pliers (see photo of fabric-working tools, Fig. 6-14).

Tight canvas will show up imperfections in the surface beneath—if not immediately, certainly when the deck has been in use for a while. Consequently, care is needed to present a

Fig. 6-14. Fabric-working tools; from left to right: upholsterer's pliers and a **cop** of sail twine, eyelet pliers and a reel of synthetic thread, two sailmaker's palms, a canvas hole punch with a punch and die for eyelets, and a group of needles.

164

good surface to the canvas. Nail heads, hard blobs of glue, and similar things may cause little lumps in the surface that will become holes under normal wear. Punch nails below the surface. Scrape and sand any unevenness. Holes and cracks should be plugged and rubbed down. Small holes filled with paint will not affect the canvas surface, but sprung plank joints or similar gaps seem to suck hollows in the canvas after a time and mar the surface. Good paint or varnish needn't be removed, but any gloss should be rubbed down.

Do not use a quick-drying paint for a canvas deck. A conventional paint that takes all day to dry is best. However, if an unprotected deck has suffered from exposure to the sun, it may be given a quick-drying coat before the paint for the canvas is applied. If it is in good shape and the grain is filled with the residue of earlier coats, the paint for the canvas may be applied directly.

With the canvas ready and trimmed as much as possible, and the tools and tacks at hand, give the deck a thick coat of paint. Tack the canvas in place, using the technique described, and work the paint into the joints. If the paint dries, soaks in, or evaporates too quickly, apply it faster. Work quickly, embedding the canvas in the paint. Besides pulling at the edges, rub down the body of the piece.

Before the paint under the canvas dries, apply a thin coat on top of the canvas; the viscosity must be light enough to allow the liquid to soak into the canvas and bond to the paint below. This should be followed with a regular coat while the lower paint is still tacky, so all of the paint applied will bond together and impregnate the canvas. The weave of the canvas showing through the paint will provide a nonslip surface.

Deck-canvas repairs, other than minor ones, involve the replacement of complete sections using methods applied to a first covering. Small tears and holes should be patched on with squares or other shapes large enough to overlap the damage by about 1 in. all around. Fray the edges of the patch by pulling out threads (Fig. 6-15A). Sand or scrape the paint around the damage to expose the canvas and remove any paint gloss. Coat the deck and the patch with an impact-proof adhesive, allow it to get tacky, and press the patch into place. The frayed edges will keep the edges of the patch from curling.

Trim larger damage areas to a rectangular hole. Make ½ in. diagonal nicks in the corners and turn the edges out. Make a

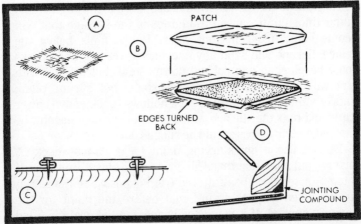

Fig. 6-15. Small holes should be patched with pieces having frayed edges to prevent curling. The hole is cut to a rectangle, the edges nicked with diagonal cuts, and the edges folded back (B) and interlocked with similar edges in the patch (C). Plastic covering that can't be bent up against a vertical side is made watertight with molding planed in the corner to accept jointing compound (D).

patch large enough to have folded edges to match the hole (Fig. 6-15B). Interlock the edges of the hole and patch, then saturate the whole thing and drive tacks through the overlaps (Fig. 6-15C).

Plastic deck coverings are fitted like canvas, but because they are fairly stiff, they are unsuitable for decks or cabin tops with much compound curvature. Stiff deck coverings that cannot be bent to follow vertical bulkhead surfaces should be covered with a quarter-round molding planed off at its cover to provide a space for jointing compound (Fig. 6-15D). Some plastics can be softened enough with heat to conform to corners and other awkward places.

Special adhesives are needed to fill holes and weld damaged edges in plastic deck coverings. Common adhesives will not hold on vinyl. Larger damage means replacement or sewing using techniques similar to those for canvas. Vinyl will not take ordinary paint. Worn surfaces will have to be revived, or matched to other work, with one of the special coatings intended for this material (often supplied in spray cans). The coatings are suitable for both flexible materials and rigid sheets, but colors are limited.

# *Ropeworking*   7

Ropes and cordage have been revolutionized in recent years by plastics and synthetic materials. Before them, rope was made of such natural fibers as hemp, cotton, manila (plant fiber), sisal, and coir (coconut fiber); all had their place aboard ships, and are still used—but to a diminishing extent. Ropes made from natural fibers look and feel hairy because of projecting ends of some of the necessarily short fibers used. However, this is no sure identification of natural ropes; some synthetics have been given the same feel for a better grip.

Hemp and manila are found in general-purpose yacht ropes. They have little stretch and are reasonably strong. Cotton, a smoother and more flexible material, is used for sheets, and ropes that have to be handled. Coir is weak, but it stretches and floats (the others tend to sink). Because of its qualities, coir was used in fairly thick sections for towing and mooring. Sisal always has been the cheap alternative to general-purpose ropes. It is rough with stiff, projecting fibers. New cotton is white; other fibers are brown, coir being the deepest shade. After use they all bleach or wear to a medium brown. The only sure way to identify them is to become familiar with samples.

Many synthetic materials are used to make rope. The general-purpose rope for halyards and anything else needed to take stress without stretching is polyester (Dacron, for example). Except where other synthetic ropes have been used for economy, polyester ropes are the ones most likely to be used in repair work. Nylon is also used for rope and is stronger than the other common material. Some people tend to use that name for all synthetic ropes, but nylon differs from nearly all other synthetics in being both elastic and capable of absorbing water. Its elasticity makes it unsuitable for halyards and most sheets, although it is sometimes used in spinnakers. It is used for towing, anchor, and mooring lines.

Other synthetics are derived from propylene, a gaseous hydrocarbon. One of these, polypropylene, looks like nylon when it's made into fine filaments. Its strength is about half that of nylon, but it has the advantage of being buoyant. Polyethylene, also in this group, is often made into coarse, stiff rope. However, synthetic fibers may be coarse or fine, tight or loose, and some are not so easily identifiable. Some are color-coded for identification, but the code is primarily used to identify their purpose on board.

Synthetic fiber ropes are always stronger than their natural counterparts. Not only are they stronger under ideal test conditions, their strength is less affected by moisture and age—and they won't rot. This means that a thinner synthetic fiber rope can replace a natural one. Of course, this advantage shouldn't be pushed too far; it makes handling easier, but there are practical considerations that make it inadvisable to use a rope as thin as strength will allow. For instance, a sail sheet less than ⅜ in. in diameter would be difficult to handle with the thinnest permissible line for the stresses involved.

How ropes are made affects their strength. Materials vary according to makers, but Appendix B should serve as an adequate guide to rope strength. Smooth synthetic ropes are made from *continuous* filaments. When shorter pieces are used to improve grip, the rope is described as *spun* or *stapled*.

Rope sizes are usually given for the diameter, but sometimes the circumference is stated in inches and fractions of an inch. Metric measurement specifies diameter exclusively. A convenient conversion for metric measurement is: the number of eighth-inches in the circumference equals the number of millimeters in the diameter; 1⅛ inches of circumference ($^9/_8$) = 9 mm diameter, for example.

Natural fiber ropes will char and burn; synthetic ropes melt before they burn—a rope, therefore, can be broadly identified by holding a match to its end.

Rope is usually made in three strands, twisted clockwise away from you as you look along the rope. Various forms of pleated rope, suit particular shipboard uses, mainly as sheets. One or two outside layers are pleated around a core of straight filaments.

## WIRE ROPE

Wire rope remained relatively unchanged over the years. At one time, *standing rigging* was made from six galvanized iron strands (to delay rust) wrapped around a hemp core; *running rigging*, from six thinner strands of galvanized steel over the same core. Galvanized steel is still used for either purpose, but saltwater-resistant stainless steel rope is more commonly used on new yachts; the construction, however, is traditional. In cross section, six circles surround a seventh of the same size, all touching to maintain the rope's shape. The most recent configuration, nineteen strands, works even better in this respect. Repairing rigging usually involves the complete replacement of galvanized wire with stainless wire.

## PRESERVATION

In a natural fiber rope, rotting can be seen as a darkening of the interior. Slight browning is acceptable, but near-black is a bad sign. Both indicate eventual failure from internal abrasion caused by sand penetrating the rope and wearing away the fibers. This effect will be apparent when the rope is sprung open. Rope may be washed with warm water and detergent. But don't rinse it with a hose—grit will be forced into the rope.

Many ropes are only strained in part of their length; a halyard is under strain when a sail is hoisted, but most of its length is coiled out of use. Much like rotating tires on a car, such a rope should be turned end for end to extend its life. The life of new natural fiber ropes can be extended by treating them with preservative against rot; but this treatment cannot cure a case of rot once it has set in. Although all synthetic ropes are inherently rot-resistant and don't require treatment with preservatives and waterproofing solutions, nylon can be soaked in a solution to reduce water absorption.

If you are worried about ants or other crawly insects climbing up mooring lines to stow away, they can be repelled by spraying or soaking the lines with bleach or a chlorine swimming-pool solution. Rats or other rodents are not so easily discouraged. They can only be held off by putting large cones around the lines, with their open bases faced shoreward: a standard big-ship precaution.

## ROPEWORKING TOOLS

Many of the tools needed for ropework are also used for canvas (Fig. 7-1). A good knife with a thin blade and several spikes ranging from an icepick to marlinespikes (to force open

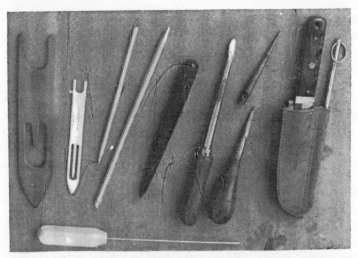

Fig. 7-1. Ropeworking tools; left to right: a knife and spike in a sheath; grooved and plain spikes; a wire-splicing spike; a wooden fid; two fids for braided rope with a pusher above; two net-making needles.

tight rope), are most important. A hardwood spike, called a *fid*, and a mallet to drive it are valuable for large ropes. Splicing and other intricate work is more easily done when sitting astride a *trestle* (a beam, as across a sawhorse), or when the work is on a bench with a strong top.

Hard-steel end cutters are needed for flexible stainless steel rope. Pliers are also needed. Wire strands can be opened for splicing by pushing in and turning a screwdriver that has been ground to a near-chisel edge. An alternative is a grooved marlinespike, but a surrogate can be homemade from a spike grooved with the edge of a grinding wheel; the strand being tucked in is guided along the groove while the spike is in place. Sailmakers' needles and palms will be needed for some *whipping* (overcast stitching).

## MAINTENANCE AND WHIPPING

Routine maintenance of natural fiber ropes, like that for natural fiber sails, involves washing out saltwater and hanging to dry. Synthetic fiber rope doesn't need this care for longevity, but washing out salt and grit is just good practice.

A stranded rope will untwist at the end if nothing is done to prevent it. Natural fiber ropes can be twisted back into shape with the right technique, but most synthetics will unravel so quickly and to such an extent that twisting them up again will be next to impossible. Dealing with rope ends will be the major part of your rope repair work.

A synthetic rope can be easily sealed by melting the end and rolling it between moistened (to avoid burns) finger and thumb. (The flame of a gas cigarette lighter leaves a cleaner finish than a match.) Professionals use an electrically heated knife that seals the rope as it cuts. But don't try to adopt this idea by warming an ordinary knife with uncontrolled heat—overheating changes the temper of the blade and may ruin its flexibility. Sealing the end is not sufficient protection. The rope should also be whipped. A temporary whipping may be made with adhesive tape used on each side of an intended cut. The rope ends can also be dipped in sealers or secured with *shrink-tubing* (plastic sleeves that contract with heat).

Whipping is done with a line very much thinner than the rope; for most ropes, strong thread will do. Traditionally, whipping line made of hemp or cotton was drawn through beeswax just before use. The beeswax waterproofed the thread and kept it in place as it was wound. Cotton or hemp whipping line might be used on synthetic ropes but it would be more logical to use synthetic whipping line; why let the whipping rot? If it is not bought already waxed, synthetic whipping should be so treated.

In what may be regarded as the "common" whipping, a few inches of line is laid along the rope and the remainder is tightly wound around it for about a dozen turns (Fig. 7-2A). The end lying along the rope is turned back in a loop, and three or four more turns are made around over it; then the unsecured end is passed through the loop (Fig. 7-2B) and dragged inside the coils of thread by pulling on the free end of the loop; the loop should pull it through to exit the coil of threads with the loop end. The operation is completed by cutting off the protruding ends (Fig. 7-2C). Skill in whipping is being able to make the final turns just loose enough to pull the end through.

An easier and firmer whipping—sometimes called *west-country whipping*—is made with a series of half-knots. Put the middle of a length of line behind the rope near its end and make a half-knot in front (Fig. 7-2D). Take the ends of the line to the back and make a half-knot there, working toward

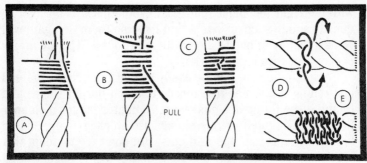

Fig. 7-2. "Common" whipping.

the end of the rope. Pull each knot as tight as possible and continue knotting back and front until the closely packed knots make a length of whipping that is no longer than the diameter of the rope. Make the last knot a square knot (Fig. 7-2E).

The strongest end is made whipping the line through the rope as well as around it, with a sail needle and a sailmaker's palm. To do it, pull most of the line through the rope leaving just enough to lay against the rope. Bind the short end tightly with coils of thread going towards the end (Fig. 7-3A). When the whipping is about as long as the diameter of the rope, loop the thread around one of the rope strands (Fig. 7-3B). Then go over the coil of thread and through it from the bottom, coming out at the top. Loop the thread around an adjacent rope strand at the top, go over, under, and through the coil again (Fig. 7-3C), and loop over the remaining strand. Secure the end by making a final pass through the coil before cutting it off.

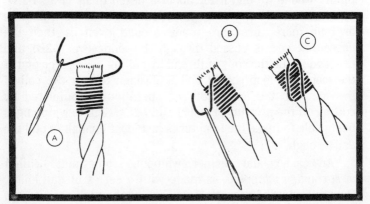

Fig. 7-3. Taking the whipping line through the rope, as well as around it, makes for the strongest end.

The whipping methods described may be applied to stranded or pleated rope, but an equivalent of palm-and-needle whipping may be used on stranded rope without a needle. It is called *sailmaker's* whipping: Open strands of rope for a short distance, loosely loop the line over one of them with both ends of the line lying between the two remaining. Pull lightly on the line until you have a long end and a very short one (Fig. 7-4A) Twist the strands back together. Hold the short end and the loop and bind the strands, coiling line tightly around the rope towards the end (Fig. 7-4B). Hold the whole thing tightly and pull the loop up and over its own strand (Fig. 7-4C). Tighten the loop by pulling the short end (Fig. 7-4D). Pull the long end through the space between strands opposite the short side of the loop and knot it in the center of the rope to the short end (Fig. 7-4E).

Oldtime sailors often put two whippings on a rope's end, one an inch or so behind the other; if the end one failed, the other would prevent the rope from untwisting into a *mare's tail*. Synthetic ropes, being slippery, are particularly susceptible to this, but sealing the end has the effect of a second whipping.

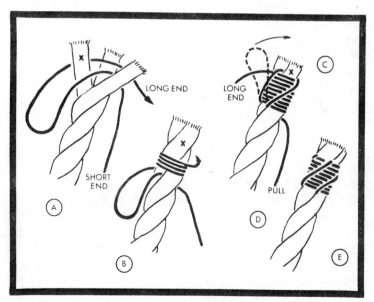

Fig. 7-4. Sailmaker's whipping produces an end similar to that in Fig. 7-3, but it can be done without a needle.

Fig. 7-5. An overhand knot (left) will prevent a rope from slipping through a hole. If a larger end is needed, a figure-eight should do (right).

## KNOTTING

Various knots may have to be made while repairing rigging. Of the thousands in knotting books, only a few will cope with all problems. In general, knots should be regarded as temporary fasteners. If cordage is to be fixed or joined permanently, a splice is better.

To stop a rope from slipping through your hand—or a hole—the knot to use is the thumb, or overhand knot (left, Fig. 7-5). If this does not produce a big enough lump in the rope, the end can be taken around the back before passing it through the loop: a figure-eight knot (right, Fig. 7-5).

The general-purpose joining knot is the *common* or sheet-bend knot. The thicker rope, if there is a difference, is bent back on itself and the other is passed through the loop (Fig. 7-6A). The end goes around the back of the loop, across the front, and through the loop it formed (Fig. 7-6B). The ends can finish on the same or opposite sides of the knot. If there is a great difference in the thickness of the ropes, or if they are slippery (synthetics), go around twice with the thin rope to make a double sheet bend (Fig. 7-6C).

To pull a thicker cord behind a thin one, as when pulling a halyard through a hollow mast, use the variation in Fig. 7-7. It

Fig. 7-6. A variation of the sheet-bend knot (A & B), is the double sheet bend (C).

Fig. 7-7. This relative of the sheet bend knot is used to pull ropes through hollow masts. The direction of pull is to the right; the ends won't get caught.

will leave the ends pointing away from the direction of pull, preventing them from getting caught; however, the knot will be weak.

The *reef*, or square knot, is the one most familiar to ropeworkers. It is only suitable for joining if it is bearing against something, as it does in joining the reef points to roll up a sail. The important thing is to twist the ends so interlocking loops are formed (Fig. 7-8). If both ends are twisted the same way, a virtually useless *granny* knot will result.

A *bowline* is the best knot for creating a large loop in the end of a rope. There are several quick ways of forming it, but the basic one is to twist a little loop behind the amount needed for the large loop, then take the end a short distance through it, from the same side the main part is on (Fig. 7-9A). Take the end around the main part of the rope, from the small loop side, and down through the small loop. Pull the end tight without losing the shape of the small loop (Fig. 7-9B).

Hitches are to attach ropes to rings and spars. The common one is the *clove* hitch; although a temporary fastening, it is satisfactory if loads on it are in opposite directions. Take one end of the rope over, under, and around the object (a spar in this example), crossing over the body of the rope (Fig. 7-10A). Wrap the end around again, working in the direction of the first crossing, and cross the end under the diagonal joining both loops (Fig. 7-10B). The clove hitch can be made before it goes on the object (Fig. 7-10C)—especially handy for hitching up to a bollard (a mooring post on a wharf).

Fig. 7-8. The square knot is also known as a reef knot; made incorrectly, it will become a useless granny knot.

Fig. 7-9. A large nonslip loop is formed with a bowline knot.

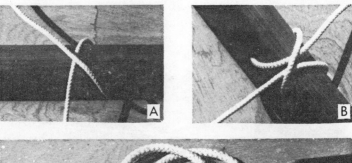

Fig. 7-10. The clove hitch, widely used on spars (A & B), can also be made beforehand (C) for throwing over bollards.

Fig. 7-11. A rope can be secured around a ring (A) with a clove hitch made to itself (B).

The best hitch for eyes and rings combines two half-hitches: The end is taken through the ring, around it, and through again (Fig. 7-11A). Then the end is used to make a clove hitch around the body of the rope (Fig. 7-11B) and the hitch is pulled tight against the ring.

A clove hitch can be easily slid up and down a spar. To attach a rope in a way that will resist slipping, as when a rope takes a load on a mast, a *rolling* hitch is used. It begins like a clove hitch, but the rope goes around and crosses over itself twice (Fig. 7-12A) before it wraps around to finally cross under (Fig. 7-12B) for the finished clove hitch.

A timber hitch is used for a temporary fastening to something relatively large, like a tree being used for mooring. It also serves as a good slip knot for pulling many loose things together. Loop the rope around the object, and then around itself; twist the end at least three times around the rope leading to the last loop (Fig. 7-13).

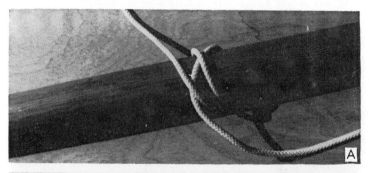

Fig. 7-12. A clove hitch will slide under a load; to prevent this, use the alternate rolling hitch: the rope takes two turns around itself initially (A). The hitch is terminated exactly like the clove hitch (B).

Fig. 7-13. A timber hitch, as its name implies, is used for temporary lashing to trees and other large objects.

A spar to be towed or lifted will require a timber hitch for strength, followed by a half hitch near the end in the right direction of pull (Fig. 7-14). A *killick bend*, with the half hitch close to the timber hitch, can be used to attach a rope to a rock as a temporary anchor.

## SPLICING

The most commonly used splice for three-strand rope is the *eye splice*: the end of the rope is spliced to form a closed loop. Making it is the most important splicing technique to be mastered for repairs to rigging.

To make an eye splice, bend enough of the end to make the loop, allowing a few inches extra—something like ten times the

Fig. 7-14. Spars are hoisted and towed with a combination of timber and half hitch; close together, the combination is called a killick bend.

diameter of the rope is about right, but better too much than too little. Untwist the surplus into strands, and put a temporary whipping around their base (Fig. 7-15A). The whipping might not be necessary for some rope, but it is especially important for synthetic ropes—they tend to unravel rapidly. Untwist the body of the rope slightly at the point where the neck of the loop will be. Poke one of the loose strands under a strand in the neck that has been lifted with a spike (Fig. 7-15B). For reference, this strand will be said to be the "front" of the splice. Take another loose strand and push it through under the neck strand adjacent to the first one used (Fig. 7-15C). Turn the splice over, exposing the unused neck strand; push the remaining loose strand under it (Fig. 7-15D). All three loose strands must be pushed through in the same direction, that is, either clockwise or counterclockwise. This is usually where the novice goes astray. If your efforts thus far have resulted in a job whose cross section looks like that in Fig. 7-15E, pull the ends together evenly. The whipping may be removed at this point.

From this stage, each end strand is taken in turn over the adjoining neck strand, into the next space and under the following strand (Fig. 7-15F). After doing this with each end strand, pull them tight, and repeat the process. This will give you a splice with each end strand passing three times under neck strands. For natural fiber ropes, this is enough; but smooth, continuous-filament synthetics have four rounds of strands tucked in. For neatness, the projecting ends can be scraped to a taper with a knife, to about half their thickness, and one more tuck made. This will give a nice looking taper to the whole splice. The splice can then be evened up by rolling it between two boards. The tucked ends around the rope should be angled the same as the neck strands, but the opposite way; almost straight tucking, as is sometimes seen, is not as strong.

An eye splice that is just a loop in rope, does not have to be made with great precision, but if it is to fit around a thimble, the tucks have to be started with care. Prepare the rope as before and loop it around the thimble. Insert the first end strand close to the thimble (Fig. 7-16). Small sizes of rope are all that are usually required on a yacht. The thimble can be removed from a loop made with small diameter rope after the first tuck is made; then the other two ends are loosely tucked,

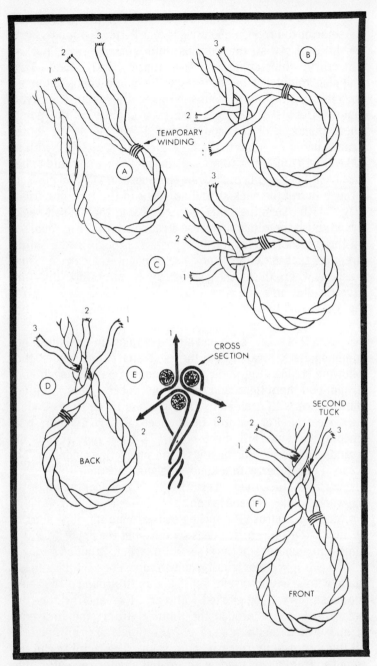

Fig. 7-15. Making an eye splice to put a permanent loop in the end of a rope. (See text for descriptions.)

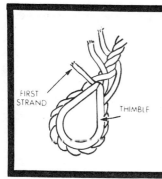

Fig. 7-16. The eye splice can be made around a thimble for extra support and protection against wear. Whether or not the thimble is removed before the job is complete, the first strand (1) must be pulled through as close to the thimble as possible.

FIRST STRAND

THIMBLE

the thimble replaced, and the three ends pulled tight before continuing tucking.

### Eye-Splicing Braided Rope

Braided (pleated) rope is being increasingly used for ease of handling, comfort and manageability. It is also more truly circular, an advantage with some winches and some other equipment. Older braided rope, pleated outside with straight yarns inside, is slowly being replaced by double-braided cordage: An outside pleated cover encloses a pleated core. The material is usually polyester or nylon. The methods of eye-splicing these ropes differ from each other, as well as from those emplyoed in eye-splicing standed rope.

Special tools are needed for splicing braided rope. For the rope likely to be met in boat repairs (up to 1 inch in diameter), there has to be a round, metal fid to suit each size. It is a rod with a tapered, rounded point and a hole in the other end (in the left side of Fig. 7-1). Marks on the fid are used as a gage. Recommended sizes are shown in Appendix C. A pushing tool (only one size needed for most ropes) goes with the fid. Some adhesive tape (masking tape will do) is needed for temporary whippings, and a crayon or pencil for marking the rope. The marlinespike and a sharp knife will also be used.

Splices can be made in single-braided rope with end strands tucked to follow the pattern of the pleat, if the pleating is fairly loose. It is better to use *lock* tucking: burying the tapered end. The end of the rope is first marked in two fid-length increments and a loop is bent at the second mark from the end. After the loop is adjusted to the desired eye size, the second mark is transferred to the opposite side of the loop. (Fig. 7-17A).

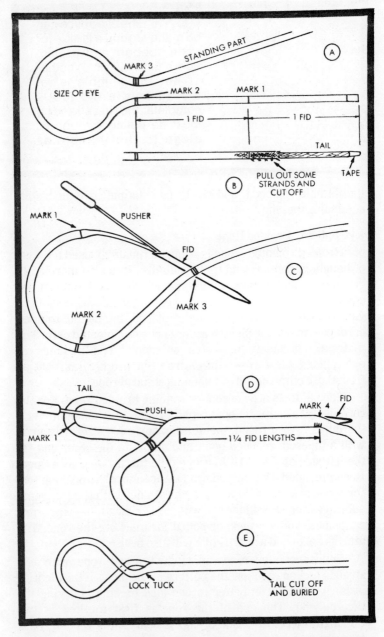

Fig. 7-17. Lock tucking: the taped end of a sigle-braided rope (without a braided core) is buried in the neck of the loop in this form of eye splice.

184

The first fid length (nearest the end) is tapered by cutting out some strands (Fig. 7-17B) and taped at its point. Jam the tapered end into the fid and use the pusher to force the fid through the rope at mark 3 (in the drawing) until mark 2 reaches mark 3 (Fig. 7-17C). Do not twist the line. Make a mark four strand intersections away from mark 3, towards the body of the rope; this will be towards the body of the second point of insertion.

Mark 1¼ fid lengths from the point of insertion, towards the body of the rope (mark 4) . Push the fid through the point of insertion. Take the end through and out at mark 4 (Fig. 7-17D). Pull the end hard to tighten the lock tuck and remove any bunching. Cut off the projecting piece. Smooth the braiding away from the eye until the taped tip disappears into the rope; the splice is complete (Fig. 7-17E). Ropes larger than ⅝ inch in diameter could be given one or two additional tucks before the end is buried.

Double-braided rope may be given an extremely neat and strong eye splice. Begin, as before, by taping the end of the rope. Make a mark one fid-length from the end, form the loop at this mark, and transfer the mark to the other side of the loop. Take the size of the loop from a thimble, if you plan to use one. Tie a slip knot five fid-lengths from the second mark, in the long side of the rope. It will prevent the braided center from moving, relative to the braided cover beyond that point. (An alternative is to push a spike through this point.)

Bend the rope sharply at the second mark (mark X in Fig. 7-18) and use a spike to open the cover and pry out the pleated core (Fig. 7-19). Pull the center completely out of the cover. Tape the end of the core. Put a mark on the core where it

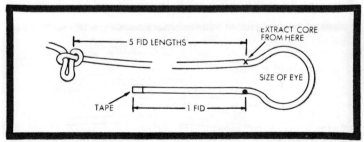

Fig. 7-18. Double-braided rope is marked off in fid lengths for an eye splice. The following six illustrations accompany directions for the splice's completion.

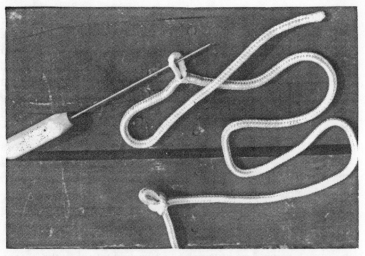

Fig. 7-19. Eye splice: Prying out the core.

comes out of the cover. (To insure there has been no slipping of the cover over the center, smooth the cover from the slip knot towards the ends before marking.)

Slide the cover back ⅓ fid-length, mark the core there, then expose a section 1⅓ fids long and mark it. Push the fid through the core at the second mark (mark 2 in Fig. 7-20). Pass the fid through the core so it just pokes out of mark 3 by bunching up or "milking" the cover behind it. Push the end of the cover into the hole in the fid and jam the end of the pusher in with it (Fig. 7-21). Push the fid through until the first mark on the cover almost disappears. Remove the tools and leave the end projecting.

Next, the core end has to be pushed through the cover. Enter the fid at the first mark in the cover and pass it through

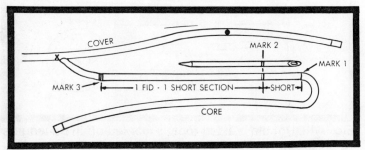

Fig. 7-20. Eye splice: entry and exit marks for the fid.

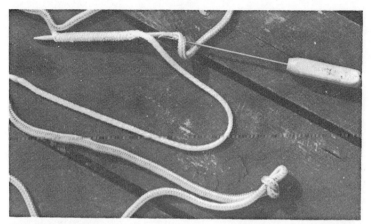

Fig. 7-21. Eye splice: pushing the cover and fid through the core.

to exit at the mark indicating the length of the loop. If the distance around the loop is more than the length of the fid, take the fid out at a convenient spot, pull it through, then reinsert it (Fig. 7-22A). Pull the core end through until it is tight. If necessary, adjust the tension in the cover end so the crossover is tight in both directions.

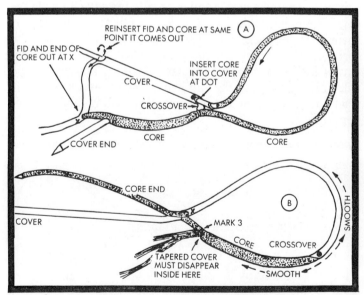

Fig. 7-22. Eye splice: (A) pulling out and reinserting the fid; (B) concealing the cover end within the core.

Fig. 7-23. Eye splice: The cover is concealed and the splice is ready for the final stage.

The end of the cover has to be made to disappear inside the loop. Cut off the taped end, unravel the braid, and cut off staggered lengths strands to achieve a taper (Fig. 7-22B). Smooth both sides of the loop away from the crossover until all the cover ends disappear into the rope at mark 3. This stage of the eye splice is shown in Fig. 7-23.

The last stage is to draw the cover over all of the core and the crossover. This is done by *milking* the cover: stroking the cover with your hand to make it slide away from the slip knot. As this is done, the center will gradually bury itself inside the cover. Continue to do this (Fig. 7-24) until the whole loop is enclosed in cover braid. Smooth the eye in the direction of the core end. Cut off the tail reasonably close to the cover, but leave a little exposed. Pull at the top of the eye and the cut end will disappear. Untie the slip knot; smooth and stretch the whole rope to even the pattern of braiding and restore appearance.

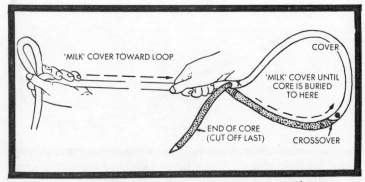

Fig. 7-24. Eye splice: "milking" the cover over the core.

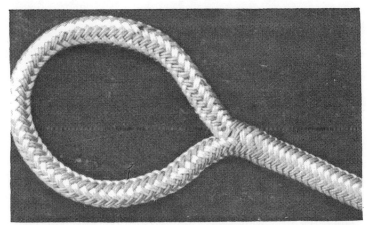

Fig. 7-25. The completed splice—seeing it at this point, could you have guessed how it was done?

Smaller ropes can be left at this stage (Fig. 7-25), but a whipping at the neck of the eye is advisable for larger ropes. A hollow or slackness will appear at the neck if the end of the core is cut off too close. It won't affect strength enough to matter if it happens, but next time allow a little more core when cutting off. If an eye has to be made in old rope, soak it in water to loosen and lubricate the fibers.

### Other Splices

A variation of eye splicing that should be used more often is the *cut* splice. It provides an eye within a length of rope—to slip over a mast head or a tiller, for instance—or the splice can be used to join two ropes. Two lengths of rope are overlapped by an amount needed for the size of loop, plus some for tucking (Fig. 7-26), then one rope is spliced into the other the same way as for an eye splice; the second is tucked into the first to complete the loop.

Fig. 7-26. The cut splice provides an eye between lengths of rope.

A common way to join two ropes the same size, or to join the parts of a rope after a damaged part has been cut out, is to use a *short* splice. The only snag with this is that it doubles the circumference of the rope, making it too large to pass through close-fitting holes. It is most useful for repairing mooring or towing lines, or making them from discarded working lines.

Allow enough untwisted strands ends for tucking and join the ropes, with the strands of one rope going between the spaces of the other rope's strands. If the rope is very loosely twisted, put a temporary whipping around the base of one rope's loose strands (Fig. 7-27A). Assuming that one rope is whipped, pull the strands of the other towards the whipping, with their base tightly against it; whip the ends you pulled, behind the first whipping (Fig. 7-27B). Take the loose ends remaining over their neighbors on the other rope, working in one direction, and then under the next strands one-over (Fig. 7-27C). Do this twice more (Fig. 7-27D). Remove the whipping. Repeat the process with the end strands of the rope first whipped; going three times the other way. The six tucks should be enough, even for slippery synthetics. You can taper the projecting ends and tuck each once more for better appearance and more security.

The *long* splice, not often needed in repair work, should be part of your repertoire. Like the short splice, it is used to join two ropes, but it does not increase the thickness of the rope at the splice. However, it consumes a lot of rope in the process. Because of this, it is more usual to replace a yacht rope, rather

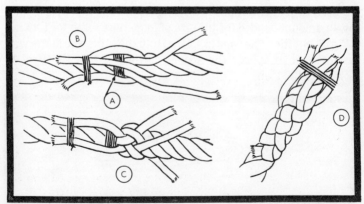

Fig. 7-27. Two ropes the same size are usually joined with a short splice.

than risking making it too short for its job by long splicing. The splice uses up something like 50 times the circumference of the rope; a rope ½ inch in diameter—about 1½ inches in circumference—would lose about 6 feet in splicing.

A long splice is begun by untwisting each end for a length about 40 times the diameter; then they are interlocked in the same way for a short plice. A strand of one end is then further untwisted at the same time its neighbor from the other end is twisted into its place. This must be done carefully so as not to disturb the natural twist and kinking of the strand being twisted. Continue until all but a few inches of it have been twisted. Repeat this action the other way with another pair of strands. The splice will look like a continuous rope with pairs of ends projecting at long intervals (Fig. 7-28A). Several ways of dealing with these ends are possible, the most satisfactory method is to separate the ends lengthwise, then hook one half of each together and tuck the thin projecting ends into the adjoining strands (Fig. 7-28B).

The *back* splice, an alternative to whipping, suffers from the same fault as the short splice, thickening the rope and making it impossible to pass it through tight spaces. However, it has the advantage of not needing whipping; it makes a good emergency treatment for a fraying line when no whipping line is available.

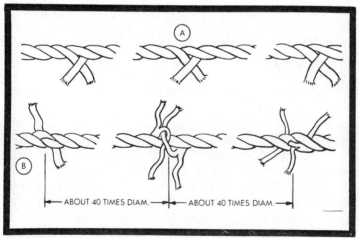

Fig. 7-28. The long splice results in three pairs of projecting strands that are halved, hooked together, and tucked in. The only drawback is the large quantity of rope consumed.

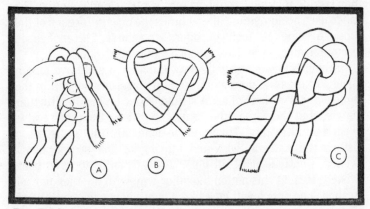

Fig. 7-29. In an emergency, it would suffice to tie the loose strands of a frayed rope (A) into a crown knot (B). The ends should later be tucked over and under strands several times (C).

To make a back splice, untwist the end strands for tucking and, for a first attempt at least, hold the rope in your left hand with the ends equally spaced (Fig. 7-29A). With your right hand, take each end counterclockwise over its neighbor (Fig. 7-29B). Pulling the ends tight, you have a *crown knot*. In an emergency this would be enough to prevent an end from unraveling wastefully. But for a complete back splice, point each end down towards the body of the rope and tuck it under a main strand (Fig. 7-29C)); then take each of the ends "over and under one" three times, as in the other splices described. Finish with a taper tuck and cut off before rolling (between boards) for neatness.

More modern ways of joining and looping wire ropes can be used instead of splices. Nearly all involve equipment to *swage* or other wise squeeze fittings. The strands of some wire rope can be put through end fittings, such as the "Norseman" wedge-action sleeves, which are tightened with wrenches. Anyone using fittings for repairs should make sure they match the wire exactly. Wire clips, either the type used to compress cables (Fig. 7-30A) or U-bolts tightened with nuts (Fig. 7-30B) are good alternatives for emergency repairs. Use at least a pair of fittings on any repair. The U-bolt type is most secure when the free end is doubled back through the bolt (Fig. 7-3C). This also puts the rough wires in a position where they are less likely to scratch hands and sails.

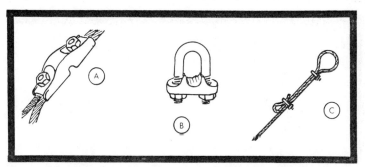

Fig. 7-30. With the necessary equipment on hand, fittings rather than splices can be used to repair wire rope. For added security, and to get rough ends out of the way, double the end back through a U-bolt (C).

The only wire splice usually required is putting an eye in seven-strand rope. The method is much the same as that used for fiber rope, but the springiness and intractability of wire makes splicing difficult if preparations are not properly made. To begin any splice in wire rope, wrap tape around the rope on both sides of the intended cut. If you haven't a pair of powerful cutters for wire, lay the rope down on an iron block and chop it, using a mallet and *cold* chisel—the kind that can withstand such treatment. If the core strand is hemp, it will be cut off; but if it is wire, it will be buried as the splice is made. A wire core strand can be easily identified as being free of spiral kinks.

The wires of each strand have to be prevented from untwisting as soon as the strand is withdrawn from the tape. Some workers dip the end into flux and then into molten solder. This is good, but the materials are unlikely to be available where most repairs are required. An alternative is to use two pairs of pliers, or a vise and pliers; grip about ¼ inch from the end and twist the exposed wires tightly together. Alternatively, use cotton thread or other fine line and temporarily whip each strand—a few turns of west-country whipping should be enough.

Most wire splices are made around thimbles. The wire is first looped around the thimble and secured with two whippings: one wound around the middle of the thimble's broadest curve; the other, in figure-eight turns around the neck (Fig. 7-31A). Handling can be simplified using a vise or clamp to hold the job upright, but the usual wire sizes shouldn't

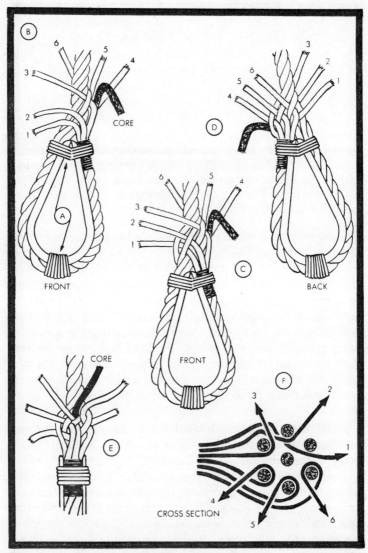

Fig. 7-31. A wire splice around a thimble must first be secured with two whippings (A). The strands are pulled through the neck of the loop on one side (B), and then on the other (C). Projecting ends (D) are pulled tight, and the splice is finished by rounding it with a mallet.

make freehand tucking too awkward. All these preparations may seem time-consuming to anyone who has not made a wire splice, but they are essential.

Pick out the core strand and turn it back out of the way of the others. Arrange the splice so that what may be regarded as the "front" has three end strands pointing across main strands (Fig. 7-31B). (Ignore the three in the back at this point.)

Lift a main strand on the front with a grooved spike, or stick in a screwdriver and twist it, after entering, then tuck the strand numbered 3 in the drawing before withdrawing the spike. Tuck No. 2 next, going in where No. 3 comes out, in the same direction, under the next strand. Follow with No. 1, this time going in the same place No. 2 did, but under two strands (Fig. 7-31C) (This is the only tuck to be made under two strands.)

Turn the splice over and identify the unused main strands. Tuck Nos. 4, 5, and 6 in turn under these in a direction that crosses the twist of the rope (Fig. 7-31D). At this stage the splice looks somewhat like a cage. Press the core strand against rope, away from the thimble (Fig. 7-32E).

Use pliers to pull and tighten each end in turn, working close to the thimble. You may have to go around doing this several times. When all the ends are about on the same plane around the rope, use a mallet or a lead hammer with a block to knock the whole thing into a tighter, round shape. You should now have one end projecting from each space (Fig. 7-31F), with the core strand standing above one of the tucked strands.

Continue as in fiber rope splicing, tucking each end over and under successive strands and across the direction of twist. Pull and shape after each of three full rounds of tucks. Cut off alternate end strands and the core strand. Tuck the remaining three ends once or twice more. Some workers make the last tucks under two strands before cutting. Knock the splice into as good a shape as possible. It is usual to wrap the bare ends with many turns of self-adhesive plastic tape. A repairer may be faced with the problem of having to pull a new wire rope through a hollow mast. This can be solved by splicing a fiber rope tail to the main wire part. An old halyard still in the mast may be used to pull a new one through after the two are seized together as compactly as possible. This may present a problem if the mast has a very confined hollow. Sometimes fittings and the double thickness of wire they hold make it through a narrow mast. If this is so, use the old halyard to pull

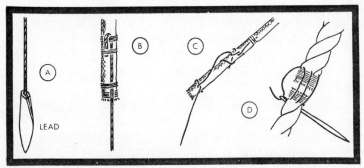

Fig. 7-32. A wire rope usually has to be pulled up through a hollow mast with a fiber rope. The fiber rope is weighted (A), dropped down the center of the mast, and attached to the wire rope in one of three ways: knotting (B), whipping (C), or sewing (D).

through a light line, which can then be used to pull through the new halyard.

If the mast is unoccupied, a weighted line will have to be dropped down through it. A piece of lead with its end hammered around the knotted end of a whipping line makes the most compact weight. (Fig. 7-32A). There shouldn't be any projecting pieces to catch on the way down. An advantage of lead is that you can fish for it with a bent wire at its exit. To best secure light line to thicker wire or fiber rope, bind them together at several points along their overlapping ends (Fig. 7-32B). An alternative is to use a rolling hitch followed by a half hitch near the end (Fig. 7-32C). It might also be possible to sew the whipped ends of both ropes together (Fig. 7-32D). If there is enough space to take a double thickness of halyard, fiber rope can be doubled back and the hauling line attached with a double sheet bend.

### Splicing Wire Rope to Fiber Rope

Fiber rope does not usually last as long as the wire rope its spliced to and may have to be replaced often. Careful unpicking will reveal the type of splice used—there are several variations. If there is little size difference between the fiber rope and the wire rope, the core strand should be cut out of the wire rope, then the outer strands paired and tucked into the fiber rope in a short splice. However, wire rope of comparable strength to its fiber rope tail will usually be much thinner, making a short splice satisfactory.

196

A neat and strong alternative method is to tuck the wire in two groups of three strands. Prepare the wire by untwisting enough for tucking. The ends of strands will have to be secured with whippings, twisting with pliers, or by soldering. Untwist alternate strands further; how much further depends on rope sizes, but 6 inches is reasonable for small halyards (Fig. 7-33A). The core strand may remain within the three untwisted strands. Temporary whippings will be needed.

Untwist enough fiber strands to extend several inches past the point where the second untwisting terminated. Mesh the ends of both together (Fig. 7-33B) and put a temporary whipping over the joint (C). The fiber rope has to be twisted over the three wire strands, but to keep down bulk, the strands should be tapered by scraping away fibers from each first.

After the fiber rope is twisted around the wire one and meshed in a second joint (D), tuck the projecting wire ends over and under the rope strands between joints (Fig. 7-33E). Do this three times at both places. Cut off the ends and bury them inside the fiber rope. Twist the remaining fiber ends around the wire rope and finish them with a firm whipping (Fig. 7-33F).

Splicing pleated fiber rope to wire rope requires a different technique. With double-braided rope, the wire is enclosed inside the fiber rope and the inner and outer braidings are

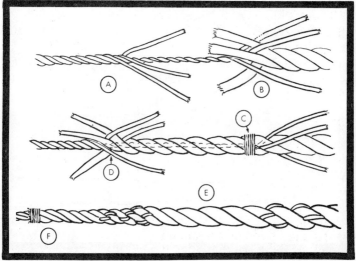

Fig. 7-33. One method of splicing wire rope to fiber rope.

tucked into the wire at two positions. Start this splice by putting a slip knot in the braided rope about 4 ft from the end and slide back the cover about 15 in. Cut 9 in. off the core (Fig. 7-34A). This leaves the cover 9 in. longer than the core, but keep it pulled back at this stage. Secure the ends of the wire strands as compactly as possible—they will not be separated in this splice. The end of the wire will go into the fiber rope so it is important to eliminate any roughness by securing the end with solder or a very tight whipping. Allow the core strand to project a few inches further than the outside strands, if you wish to get a tapered effect and provide some rigidity for the fiber rope mext to the start of the splice.

Push the wire rope into the braided fiber core. Tape or whip the fiber rope, leaving enough for tucking (Fig. 7-34B).

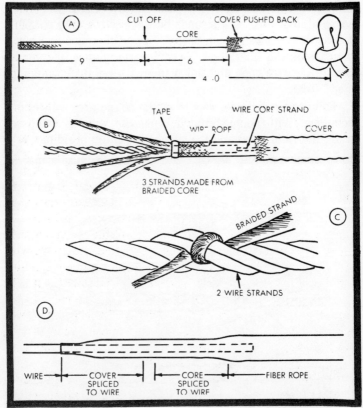

Fog. 7-34. Wire rope can be whipped and sealed at the end and then pushed into the braided core of a fiber rope.

Untwist the braided core end and twist the strands into three. Tuck these into the wire for 3 to 4 inches. Wrap the paired strands around two wires at each tuck (Fig. 7-34C). The strand may go around more than once. Tuck in this way over and under pairs of wires, tapering the strands as you progress.

Next "milk" the cover braiding over the spliced part. Work all the slack out of it. Temporarily tape or whip over the point where the inner tuckings finish. Unbraid the cover and twist its strands into three strands. Tuck the three strands into the wire rope as you did the fiber core strands, tapering as you progress. This completes the splice (Fig. 7-34D).

## NET REPAIRS

Nets are used for fishing and as racks and bags to hold small items and sails. Netmaking is often regarded as something of a mystery, yet it is only the systematic repetition of sheet bend knotting. Repairing a net involves working in a new piece of line with more of these knots in the manner of the original work. The first job, then, is to examine existing knots and turn the net so that the point where the knots cross is in the front and above interlocks (Fig. 7-35A). Before you begin the knotting, push a rod through a row of meshes above the damaged part. There is no need for special tools for just a few meshes. Trim away the damaged line, cutting close to knots. Untie upper meshes to leave loops. Tie the new line to the mesh above and to the left of the open area (Fig. 7-35B), using a sheet bend or any other convenient knot. Use your fingers as a gage to regulate mesh size, and take the end up through the mesh to the right (Fig. 7-35C). Hold the bottom of the mesh and take the end of the line around the back of the mesh and then under itself in the front (Fig. 7-35D). Pull tight and move on to the next mesh. Be careful; if you let the loop slip from behind the mesh, the knot will be distorted when you tighten it. The opening may have to be trimmed so you can go down to the side of a mesh to start another row to finish across lower meshes going to the left (Fig. 7-35E). You may have to turn the work over or upside-down occasionally to make knotting more convenient.

It would be tedious to work in this way over a large area with a long line. For larger areas, two netmaker's tools will be needed: a mesh stick—merely a piece of wood with rounded edges and corners, half a mesh wide (Fig. 7-36A); and a

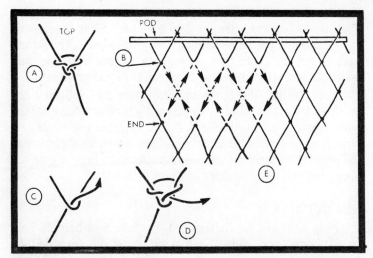

Fig. 7-35. A small net repair can be made with simple hand knotting, once the net is faced the right way according to previous knotting.

needle, narrow enough to pass through the meshes. The line is wrapped around the needle from alternate sides and through the forked end (Fig. 7-36B).

The mesh stick is held to the bottom of mesh and the line is taken down in front of it and up behind the mesh (Fig. 7-36C), where it is held by the thumb to the edge of the mesh stick. The needle then goes behind the mesh, and through the loop that is now being held by the thumb (Fig. 7-36D).

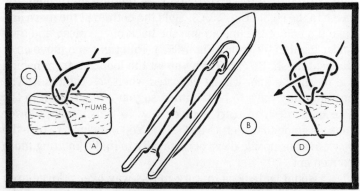

Fig. 7-36. Extensive damage to netting will require special but simple tools: a mesh stick (A) and a needle (B). (See text for the knotting technique.)

# Equipment System Repairs

**8**

Modern yachts carry mechanical and electrical equipment, radio and navigation gear, and domestic facilities comparable to those found ashore. Unless the owner particularly wants to go back to the simplicity of the basic craft of less than a century ago, he has to live with these complexities and learn to deal with at least some of them when they go wrong. The average owner would be ill-advised to open up electronic equipment that ceases to work, or delve too deeply into the inner workings of a faulty motor, unless he is particularly adept in these areas. But in an emergency he may have no alternative but to try his own efforts.

A good seaman anticipates what might go wrong and knows what to do if it happens. This necessitates a sort of "bootstrap" attitude; at sea you have to rely more on your own resources than you would when moored to a dock. Alternatives to normal repair procedures should always be kept in mind. Whenever possible, keep substitutes ready so the defective articles can be repaired ashore. A second battery and some duplicate wiring would provide insurance against electrical failure. A second fuel tank with its own piping, filters, and controls could be lifesavers if the main system became choked with sediment during a rough passage.

## TOOLS

Damaged equipment could call for a large range of tools—some quite ordinary, and others very specialized. Some equipment will have to be repaired with tools devised by the manufacturer. For instance, removing the flywheel to get at the ignition system of some outboard motors requires a factory-made extractor. Complex equipment is usually supplied with a handbook listing special tools. Obviously, if an owner wants to be able to deal with jobs that would otherwise have to go to an expert, he must be prepared to buy some special tools. Their cost has to be weighed against the possible frequency of their use; it might be more economical to employ the expert on the rare occasions such repairs have to be made.

For special mechanical work, the tools suggested for metal repairs will have to be expanded to a larger variety. Screwdrivers in many sizes and with several types of tips are needed. A handle with interchangeable bits makes for economy of space, but the bits can be easily lost on a boat. There will be occasions when a short screwdriver is needed, or one with an angled end to get at an inaccessible screw. A watchmaker's screwdriver set will be needed if instruments have to be opened.

A socket wrench set with ratchet and brace handles, and sockets to suit screws from a ¼ to ½ inch, will deal with most ordinary nuts and bolts. The only snag is the large number of pieces to lose. Double-ended wrenches, or the type with one open end and a ring at the other, are the expert's choice, but you need a larger variety of them. For the small nuts and bolts in instruments, get a kit of small wrenches and a few nutdrivers. Special extractors are needed for broken studs or screws lodged in casting holes that don't go all the way through. They are available in kits of several sizes, each with a steep, left-handed thread on a tapered end. To use one, drill a hole in the broken fastener that is slightly larger than the small end of the extractor. Force the extractor in and turn it counterclockwise with a wrench. After the extractor is tight, further turning should unscrew the fastener without damaging the hole in the casting.

Several adjustable wrenches in addition to those in the basic kit are a good standby, particularly the type of which locks on top the work. Apart from their intended job, they can be used as small vises.

There will have to be a certain amount of hitting when assembling or dismantling most equipment. To avoid damaging a hammer use pieces of wood between it and the work. Two or three hammer sizes are advisable. It is often better to control a hammer blow by using a punch between the hammer and the object. Keep several sizes, and a few of soft metal, such as brass, to avoid damaging surfaces. The variety of files kept will depend on how much work you anticipate, but have at least enough to file and fit stock items. Fine work in electrical equipment and instruments can be done with a small needle file.

For occasional electrical wiring repairs, stripping can be done with a knife, but a proper wire stripper makes insulation removal much easier. Pliers with long, round, and other special noses are needed for many electrical jobs.

Much electrical work will entail soldering. Solder is a mixture of lead and tin, melted and allowed to harden to join metal parts. A small electric iron is ideal; but out of reach of outlets, an old-fashioned flame-heated iron will have to be used. To prevent oxidation of the surfaces as the joint is being made, *flux* has to be used. For general soldering, paste or liquid flux will work, but it has to be cleaned off to prevent corrosion later. If this is impractical, there are special fluxes for small electrical connections, sometimes as a core in the solder itself.

To make a soldered joint, first scrape both parts shiny. Heat the iron until it will melt the solder on contact. If you're using a flame for heat, clean the iron by dipping it in flux—just a quick touch. An electric iron will remain clean enough without flux. Apply flux to parts to be joined if there is none in the solder. Bring the parts together and touch them with the iron, allowing a short time for the heat to spread, and touch the iron's tip with solder (Fig. 8-1); the solder should melt and

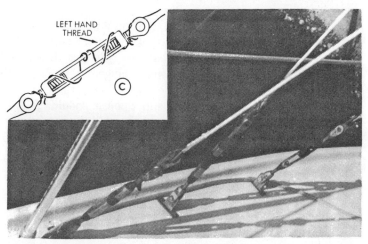

Fig. 8-1. Turnbuckles can be prevented from becoming loose by winding wire around them in a direction opposite their tendency to turn (inset), followed by taping.

flow over the joint. Beware of overdoing it—pull the solder away. Hold the parts together until the solder hardens.

A basic hacksaw frame will serve most sawing purposes. A long one is more generally useful than a short one. Have a good supply of blades of different types. High tensile steel will keep sharp longer, but it's brittle and often breaks before wearing out. Fine teeth are needed for cutting tubes. There are special blades for some metals. A lot of fatigue can be avoided by using the correct blades for the metal being cut.

While welding equipment may be used ashore by the expert, a blowtorch is probably the most an amateur can manage. It can be used to anneal metal or soften it for bending, soldering, or brazing.

## MECHANICAL DECK GEAR

There are a number of mechanical devices in a yacht, such as winches for anchor and ropes, reefing gear to roll up sails, and tackle for handling sheets. Maintenance for this gear is largely preventive. Plastic bearings do not require lubrication, but metal bearings should be oiled regularly. Ball and roller bearings are likely to have grease points for a gun similar to that used on cars. The special oils and greases manufactured for use afloat are preferable to general-purpose lubricants. If a bearing can be easily dismantled, open it up and examine it occasionally. Rust-prone equipment should not be allowed to remain unlubricated too long.

Some winches, reefing gear, and similar equipment is prevented from reversing direction with a *pawl* and pinion gear. The pawl rides over the gear going in one direction, clicking as it slaps the teeth; but when the gear reverses, the pawl gets caught in the teeth. This action will eventually cause the pawl to become blunted and slip when it shouldn't. But replacement can be forestalled by occasional filing.

Some turnbuckles cannot be locked; they can be prevented from accidental loosening by securing with wire. But the wire should be wound around them taken in a direction that will pull on it if parts try to slacken (inset, Fig. 8-1). The wired turnbuckle should be taped. Shackles—stirrup-like, U-shaped fastenings—without a locking arrangement will also undo themselves. Sometimes the end of the thread can be lightly tapped to form a rivet (Fig. 8-2A). This is particularly important with an anchor shackle; being under water, its condition can't be observed.

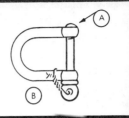

Fig. 8-2. Shackle bolts can be secured by tapping the threaded end into a rivet (A) and tying the eye end to the shackle (B).

Modern blocks (pulley casings) are better but more complicated than older, rope-strapped wooden ones. Although each is nicely engineered, the bearing needs packing with grease. And there is still a risk that wear will cause a rope to slip off the sheave. Sheet metal *shims* can be fixed on each side of the rope inside the housing to make the gap small enough to prevent the rope from coming adrift.

In some sailing craft, the main sheet and the various slides and locking devices need to be examined often. Sometimes equipment as manufactured is not as smooth as it should be. Make sliding parts run freely by filing burrs or sanding and polishing mating surfaces before lubricating. Ordinary oil and grease should not be allowed to come into contact with sails. Paraffin wax is a good lubricant between plastic and metal parts that slide against each other. Graphite may also be used, but a piece of candle rubbed where needed should be adequate.

Replacement material for plastic windows and transparent covers often comes with paper lightly attached to both sides. Leave this on as long as possible—it provides a surface for laying out cuts and protects the plastic. The plastic may be cut with a saw. Hand tools are preferable to power tools, which sometimes generate enough heat to fuse the cut surfaces. If the material is to be fitted in a plastic molding, bevel the edges slightly by sanding or filing. Fitting will be easier if the molding and plastic are lubricated with soapy water.

Before polishing an edge or removing a surface scratch, break down the surface with successively finer abrasives. Follow filing with a fairly coarse abrasive paper, then one or two finer grades, making sure that each stage removes the scratches of the previous one. The special polishes obtainable from plastics suppliers, usually in two parts, can be supplied with pumice powder or scouring powder used on a wet cloth.

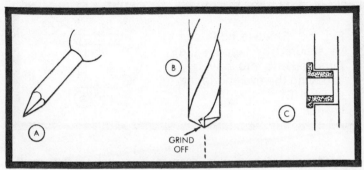

Fig. 8-3. Use a triangular spike (A) to make a dent for holes to be drilled in transparent plastic. Drill bits have to be modified for holes over $^3/_{16}$ inch wide (B). Insert a grommet (C) in the hole, and a washer over it, before using a screw.

This should be cleaned off and followed by a metal-polish finish. If you plan to use a power polisher, it must be clean. Any trace of previous metal polishing will soil the plastic. Keep the plastic moving and do not press too hard—the heat generated may cause the surface to soften and get rough.

Plastic can be drilled with a bit and hand brace after a small dent is made with the point of a triangular spike (Fig. 8-3A). Use moderate pressure. A power drill can produce so much heat that the plastic will soften, grip the drill, and crack. Ordinary metalworking drills may be for holes up to about $^3/_{16}$ inch, but larger holes require special drills with steep flutes at the tip of the bit, However, an ordinary drill can be altered for this by grinding its cutting edges upright (Fig. 8-3B). Transparent plastic should not be screwed directly to wood. Make oversize holes first to allow a little movement; put washers under the screw heads, and plastic grommets in the holes (Fig. 8-3C). Do not tighten the screws excessively. The grommets can be used again for other repairs.

## OUTBOARD MOTORS

The causes of failure in an outboard motor which otherwise has had a history of smooth operation are usually lack of fuel or lack of spark. Check for fuel in the carburetor. This can be done if the filter has a transparent cover. If there is no fuel at this point, maybe you forgot to keep an eye on the tank. Sometimes fuel starvation is merely caused by a stopcock left closed. If it is a remote tank, the air vent has to be opened and fuel pumped by hand to fill the carburetor. If a lack of fuel is not evident, go on to ignition parts.

Remove a spark plug and examine it. The end should be reasonably clean and dry. There should be nothing across the gap. Gage the gap as specified for the motor. If you have doubts about the plug, replace it and have the old one serviced. Scraping and brushing it yourself should only be considered if there is no alternative. With the lead connected, hold the loose plug by its insulation (to avoid shock), and touch the metallic portion of its body to the metal of the cylinder; turn over the motor, either by hand or with the electric starter. You should see a spark between the points of the plug.

If the motor refuses to start after several attempts, it is likely the plug is so wet with the fuel/oil mixutre that it is not sparking. A plug may be washed off with pure gasoline (without oil). It may be wiped dry, but leaving it exposed to air for awhile is usually sufficient. For fast drying, burn off the gasoline with a flame. Before replacing the plug, turn the engine over to blow out the excessively rich mixture.

Satisfactory ignition depends on heavy wire, proper insulation, and tight connections. Doubtful cable should be replaced. Spray connections and insulation with a moisture-resistant, nonconductive sealer, preferably transparent.

If there is still no spark, there may be a fault in the distributor or magneto. Look at contact points and consult the handbook for settings. If the points are fairly far gone, replace them. If not, file and reset them. Also, inspect the case and other insulation for hairline cracks. If you see any, replacement is the only cure. Use a spray on these parts too.

Some two-stroke outboard motors are more fussy than others about the correct mixture of oil and gasoline. If fuel reaches the carburetor and there is a spark, try a complete change of fuel after emptying the carburetor, and be careful to get the mixture right. If the engine starts after the carburetor has been pumped full by hand, then subsequently dies, suspect the engine-driven pump. (This rarely fails, so check everything else in the fuel system before opening the pump.) Take the fuel line off the carburetor, pointing it where escaping fuel can do no harm, and turn the motor over to see if fuel can be forced out. If it is, the pump is working. Next, check the fuel filter. This could be so choked that not enough

Fig. 8-4. Removing a propeller; a wood block is positioned to prevent it from hitting the rudder post. The propeller boss is being loosened by heat expansion with a blowtorch.

fuel is getting through. Wash the filter element in gasoline. See that all the parts of the carburetor are tight. Water in the fuel line might be stopping the motor, or an air leak in the carburetor might be affecting the mixture enough to stop it. Experience will show how much choking is needed to start the motor from cold, but some motors require that the choke be returned to normal almost as soon as the motor starts; otherwise, the excessively rich mixture will stop the motor.

In many motors, a lower unit houses the water pump as well as the gears. In the normal, water-cooled motors, a jet of escaping water acts as a check to see that water is circulating. If this stops without soon starting again, stop the motor—it could overheat. Examine the water intake for leaves or other obstructions blocking it. Sometimes stopping the motor is all that is needed to free the water system. It is unusual for the water pump itself to develop a fault, so check everything else thoroughly before dismantling it.

The gearbox is filled with oil. It is unlikely to cause trouble, but it should be topped off occasionally, according to the motor handbook; usually oil has to be forced in until it comes out of an overflow hole. Replace all screws securely, remembering to include the washers.

Many modern motors have slipping clutch arrangements to protect the gears and cylinder block when the propeller hits something. There is nothing the owner can do to these, but other motors rely on shear pins that can be replaced. Basically, the propeller is held on by a nut or cap that is secured with a cotter pin. With this removed (Fig. 8-4), and the propeller slid off, a pin can be seen going through the shaft and into a recess in the propeller: the shear pin. This pin transmits motive power to the propeller; when the propeller strikes an obstruction, the pin shears off so the shock is not transmitted to the motor. A stock of spare shear pins should be carried, but if there are none available in an emergency, a get-you-home idea is to reassemble the pin by moving the piece that was in the middle to one end (Fig. 8-5). This will only provide drives to one side of the boss (the grooved shaft end), but if acceleration is curbed, it could take the boat a few miles.

Increased vibration may be due to a damaged propeller. Filing away nicks in the edges of blades might help a minor case. But if the blade is buckled, there is no satisfactory way to fix it without elaborate equipment; replacement will be necessary.

If the motor is a four-stroke powerplant, troubleshooting will be basically similar to that for an inboard motor. If the motor runs on kerosene as well as gasoline, the carburetor will have to be drained of kerosene if it stops unintentionally and is not restarted immediately. Summarizing some snags and their remedy:

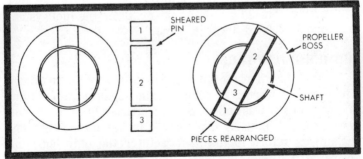

Fig. 8-5. You could limp home with a broken shear pin by rearranging the parts to provide drive to at least one side of the propeller boss.

## Failure to Start

1 Check the fuel supply. See that the vent screw is open, the hand pump is operable, and all fuel connections are correct and tight.

2 Check battery voltages. Try the hand starter. Charge or replace the battery.

3 Check for fouled spark plugs.

4 If there is no spark, check the ignition wires and insulation; check the coil and distributor.

5 The carburetor floods: Check the float for leaks; set the fuel level, either by markings in the carburetor or by the handbook.

## Motor Starts, Then Stops or Misfires

1 Check the air vent on the tank; look for water in the line. Suspect an incorrect fuel/oil mixture, that the choke is set too long, or that the carburetor fuel lever is incorrect.

2 Inspect the plugs for wear. Is the magneto or distributor clean and set correctly?

3 See if insulation, particularly around ignition wiring, is sound and dry.

4 The motor may be overheating; check water circulation.

## Misfiring

1 Look for something loose or moving where it shouldn't.

2 Check for an overrich mixture, particularly at low speeds.

3 Examine distributor points for dirt and wear, the ignition switch for worn parts, and the timing gear for slippage.

4 Check for obstructions or drops of water in the fuel system. Should you discover any, drain the fuel system and wash out dirt with gasoline.

## SUBMERGED MOTORS

If an outboard motor is dropped in the water, its treatment will depend on whether or not it was running or not at the time and how long it was submerged. Unfortunately, if the motor was running it is likely that something was bent or broken, making its return to the manufacturer the only hope for recovery. If it was not running and was recovered quickly, there is a good chance it can be made to run with little difficulty.

Many manufacturers include first-aid instructions for a drowned motor in their handbooks; broadly, the treatment is as follows:

Stand the motor upright (ashore), take off the cover and remove the spark plugs. Turn it over while the gear shift (if any) is in neutral. This should force out any water in the cylinder. If the fuel tank has been affected, empty it, and clean it and the fuel lines with gasoline. Clean out the carburetor. Place the motor on something rigid. Try to start the motor—if it starts, stop it immediately. Mount it on the boat and use it at a moderate speed for about 30 minutes. This should dry parts out of reach.

When it will not start, it is likely that the electrical system is too wet to function. Examine the plugs for moisture. If the contacts are wet, dry them and the cylinder. Apply a little oil around the plug holes. Open the distributor, wipe off any water, and dry it with warm air. A condenser is liable to be the first part to suffer from wetting and will probably have to be replaced. With the electrical gear dry and the flywheel cover replaced, try another start. If this is unsuccessful, get the motor to an expert quickly.

Some manufacturers recommend that you just drain off of as much water as possible and give it to them to do the rest. Others ask that the cylinders be opened by removing the plugs, and drained. Again, consult your instruction book and do what the maker suggests. It may mean the difference between scrapping the motor and having it to use again.*

## INBOARD MOTORS

The majority of inboard motors are basically the same as automobile engines. However, most marine engines do not get the hard, long use the average car engine has to withstand. Consequently, a boat motor can be expected to have a long life before it suffers from the wear and troubles associated with car engines. Because of this, when first investigating a breakdown, suspect the auxiliary gear before the motor proper. Most inboard motors are four-stroke machines, having four or more cylinders. A few small motors are two-strokes. Troubleshooting them is similar to the procedure described for outboard motors.

---

* For more information on outboard motors, refer to TAB book no. 727 "Complete Guide to Outboard Motor and Repair", by Paul Dempsey ($6.95 paperbound and $9.95 hardbound).

Normal boat motions can shake up water and dirt in the fuel tank, causing a failure to start or erratic running—something you may not have thought of when you checked the fuel and spark at rest. Despite your great care in fueling, water can accumulate from condensation and settle in the tank. If the tank has a removable sump filter, take it out and drain it into a container to remove any water. Clean the filter with fuel. There should be a separate filter near the carburetor. Examine the carburetor and adjacent filter; wash out any dirt, and blow out the jets with an air hose.

On the electrical side, test and clean plugs, or replace if necessary. There is more high-voltage wiring in inboard motors than on outboards, entailing more thorough examination. See that connections to the coil and distributor are good, and that insulation is in good shape. Coat everything with a protective spray. The ignition switch is sometimes overlooked as a part that conducts electricity to the plugs; see that nothing there is loose and that the contacts are good.

The distributor is a common source of electrical trouble when poor overall performance is the complaint. The cap should be in perfect condition, without chips or cracks. The rotor should also be perfect. Examine the metal end for burns. Both parts can be replaced cheaply as a preventive measure. The distributor points may need cleaning, but they should be replaced if pitted. If they are, reset them with a feeler gage. Test again after about 10 hours of use.

Internal lubrication is unlikely to give trouble unless the level in the sump is allowed to become dangerously low. Check the level with the dipstick. It is unlikely that dirty oil will stop an engine, but it will cause wear. If the oil has to be changed, warm up the engine first, then drain the thin warm oil into a container. Change the oil filter too. External parts must have adequate lubrication, but don't overdo it around electrical equipment; oil insulates electrical contacts and stops them from working.

Some motors have water pumps with a filter in the inlet valve, as well as a protective grill outside. Check that the grill and filter are clear to prevent overheating. All valves in the water system should be open. If the water pump has a belt drive, see that it is tight enough not to slip. Some pumps are fed lubricant from an oil cup. If it is not filled, the pump shaft may seize.

Throttles and transmissions are remotely controlled on most inboards. If they fail to function correctly, almost certainly it will be due to a stretched cable or a loose fitting. Working back along a remote control will usually uncover the trouble. Stretch is usually adjusted by setting the engine end of the control to neutral and altering the cable casing with a screw until the control lever is also in neutral. If looseness is the trouble, readjust and tighten the locknut, if any. If there is no locknut and one cannot be fitted, use one of the screw-locking compounds. Sticking cables may be loosened with a penetrating oil. A mixture of graphite and oil allowed to run through casings will leave a deposit of lubricating graphite after the oil has dried out.

Because marine engines differ, it is better to follow their individual handbook instructions than to rely on general directions. Treat the maker's instructions as part of the engine equipment.

## STERN GEAR

Although inboard motor gearboxes merely give FORWARD-NEUTRAL-REVERSE, they need maintenance similar to that for car gearboxes. Keep it topped with the correct oil and change the oil when you change the engine oil. Many modern installations have a drive shaft going through the transom. This should need little attention except the lubrication specified in the maker's handbook.

Trouble often comes from misalignment between the drive shaft and motor. This can only be tested when the boat is afloat. Loosen the coupling between the engine and shaft, and check to see if the parts are the same distance apart with a feeler gage. The method of realignment will depend on the installation: you must either pack the engine supports or reposition shaft supports. Errors in alignment cause loss of power.

Most shafts rely on a box to prevent leaks. It is unlikely that this will need repacking; but if more is needed, use graphite-impregated packing, cut in a ring to fit around the shaft. Tighten the nuts that compress the packing only slightly. Overtightening will cause stiffness.

Unusual vibration could be due to loose brackets at the outboard end of the drive shaft. Check this by attempting to shake the shaft. The shaft log or stern tube may loosen and cause leaks or vibration. It is usually bedded in a compound which compresses to allow the tightening of nuts.

## STEERING GEAR

A breakdown in the steering system of an outboard motor boat is best dealt with by disconnecting the gear and steering with an emergency tiller. There should always be a way of fitting a tiller to a rudder as a second means of steering. A fault in some older cable-steering installations was pulleys or sheaves too small in diameter. Eighth-inch wire rope should be used with 2 in. sheaves; thicker wire needs proportionately larger wheels. Forcing wire around small pulleys causes it to fray. A short length of new wire can be joined in with interlocking loops gripped by wire clamps, if the joints do not have to pass around sheaves; but the only satisfactory long-term repair is to replace the cable completely.

## DOMESTIC FACILITIES

Liquefied petroleum gas used for cooking may be butane or propane in colder climates—it functions at a very low temperature. Butane ceases to flow at about 32°F. The installations for both are identical. Great care should be taken in finding and fixing suspected gas leaks. The gas is heavier than air and will settle in the bilges. A passage of air through the bilges may blow it out, but beware of using an electric motor in the bilges—a spark may explode the gas. Using a vacuum cleaner set to blow, with only the tube going into the bilges, would be a safe way to eliminate the hazard.

The gas cylinder should be on the deck, or in a compartment that only opens at the top and has a vent at the bottom leading to the side of the boat. Although flexible tubes are used with some shore installations, it is better to use stainless steel or seamless copper tubing afloat. Where some flexibility is needed, as where the tube joins the regulator on the gas cylinder, there can be several coils in the tube.

Joints are usually made between tubes and equipment with a type of connector that compresses an inner part on the tube. Leaks can be spotted by brushing a soap solution or liquid detergent on the joint; bubbles will indicate leaks. Apply a coat of jointing compound when assembling tubing and connectors, particularly when remaking a joint. Compounds supplied by the gas equipment makers are preferable to general-purpose compounds because they won't be affected by gas. Rubber should not be used in any form in connection with gas equipment.

A gas stove or heater burns a mixture of gas and air. If the flame burns yellow, is extinguished, or moves away from the outlet holes when turned up, the mixture is wrong. Turn the screw or a nut controlling the air and gas flow until the flame burns blue when fully on.

Alcohol and kerosene stoves burn with a poor flame when the fuel is dirty or the jets are clogged. Some equipment has a built-in pricker to clean the hole by turning a knob below the jet. If not, there should be a separate fine wire pricker on a handle. Do not attempt to clear the jet with anything else. Damage to the jet will cause an uneven flame. The nipple containing the jet unscrews and can be replaced. Some appliances require a special wrench, which should be carried on board with spare nipples.

If the pump of a kerosene tank supplying a stove will not build up pressure, remove the handle assembly and dip the plunger in engine oil to prevent air leakage. Replace the plunger later.

Gasoline stoves work much like kerosene types; similar attention must be given to their jets. Only lead-free gasoline should be used. A small amount of gumming up caused by leaded fuel may be cleaned off with unleaded gasoline, but excessive running on too much leaded fuel may cause performance to deteriorate to the point where nothing can be done to correct it.

## WATER SYSTEMS

The domestic water system in a boat may have metal pipes with compression-coupled joints. Plastic pipes are usually joined by pushing the pipes over a metal part and squeezing with a clip. A push-on joint, without a clip, is inadvisable. Plastic tubes in several sizes, and clips to suit them, will take care of most repairs. After a few seasons of use, plastic tubes may collect algae on the inside. One way to remove it is to flush it out several times with a strong denture cleaner solution. This can also be used inside tanks.

Leaking pumps, faucets, and other water equipment can usually be cured by tightening. If a new washer is required and is not immediately available, turn over the old one to provide a temporary cure. Pump diaphragms are usually plastic or rubber-coated fabric. Keep a piece of similar material in your kit. It can also be cut to make washers, gaskets, and packings.

Sanitation on board is becoming complicated. Equipment that includes holding tanks, softening solutions, chlorinators and other contrivances instead of the straight-through-the-hull arrangements of former years, needs a handbook. Repairs should be restricted to tightening joints and lubricating where necessary. Other malfunctions should only be dealt with if the system is understood, or there is a detailed handbook at the ready. If necessary, "bucket-and-chuck-it" may have to be resorted to temporarily.

Bilge pumps vary, but most have a capacity to pass solid matter of limited size as well as water. However, articles can block valves. About the most you can do in the way of a repair is to open the pump to remove a matchstick or other small object jamming a valve open. If a metal-to-metal joint has to be opened, smear grease on it to prevent leakage when reassembling. Airtightness on the suction side is most important. Failure to suck water may be due to air leaking into a loose joint or broken pipe between the bilges and the pump. A good filter at the suction end can prevent trouble, if it is kept clean. Filters with large holes won't get clogged, but they allow solid matter through unless a large wire cage is put over the end of the pipe.

## ELECTRICAL EQUIPMENT

The battery, as a source of electricity aboard ship, is a vital item. Most small craft use lead-acid automotive types. They are satisfactory, providing they are properly maintained. A lead-acid battery will slowly lose its charge when not in use. If left fully discharged, it will soon become useless.

If there are doubts about a battery, check the electrolyte in each cell with a hydrometer: a bulb on a transparent tube is squeezed to draw up liquid to a level indicated by a floating ball—the float level indicates the state of charge. The indication may be given as GOOD, BAD, etc., but if the *specific gravity* is marked in figures, fully charged should read 1.250—1.270; half charged, 1.170—1.190; and nearly discharged, 1.090—1.110. The electrolyte should just cover the plates in the battery. Use distilled water rather than drinking water, if the level is low. In an old battery, one cell may read much lower than the others; this indicates failure and tells you it's time for battery replacement. Once a battery has been fully charged, and it is not to be used, a slow charge for about 12 hours every month will keep it in order.

Alkaline batteries have advantages over lead-acid types for use afloat, but they are more expensive. An alkaline battery will not self-discharge like a lead-acid type. It will also last longer and can be left only partly charged for long periods without deteriorating. The electrolyte should be kept fully charged, but if it is neglected, the effect will not be serious.

Boat batteries supply 12 or 14 volts of direct current (dc). Because the voltage is low, any losses along the way, in the form of poor connections or wire that is too thin, will be serious. Even in a small boat, voltage "drop" due to small diameter wiring or faulty connections could be enough to prevent equipment from working properly. If there is an obvious loss of power, check connections for corrosion. Scraping all mating surfaces may be all that is needed. If a device is permanently wired and will not have to be moved, solder electrical connections to prevent loss from gradual corrosion. Strands of flexible wiring sometimes break inside the insulation. This can be checked by attaching a wire known to be good across the suspected wiring. If the light brightens or the device works better, the fault has been found.

It is unwise to try to use the metalwork on a boat as an electrical conductor. Use positive and negative wires everywhere. Cable dealers can supply charts showing recommended cable sizes for various purposes. It is always a good policy to use a size larger than recommended to minimize drops in voltage. Faulty insulation will soon cause trouble in a damp atmosphere. Rubber insulation can become porous and leak; where possible, replace it with plastic insulation. Insulation on the verge of giving out can be temporarily repaired with insulating tape, but the whole line should be replaced as soon as convenient. A few *wire nuts* are worth having in the repair kit to splice in new lengths of wire. Merely twisting wire ends together and wrapping them with insulating tape is just for emergencies. Solder whenever you can.

Electrical circuits should be protected by fuses or circuit breakers; batteries should be connected to wiring through a double-pole switch for disconnection when the boat is out of use. Cabin craft usually have a panel with switches and fuses.

If alterations are made, or new equipment is wired in, be careful that positive and negative are not switched when you reconnect things. It is usual for positive wires to have red insulation; negative, black; and ground, green or green-and-yellow.

Power equipment, such as motors, pumps, and generators, should have their metal casings grounded to the engine. Although ground wires should not be carrying current, they should be at least as large as those that do. Grounding in this way is safer and may reduce interference with radio gear.

If a short-circuit is suspected, turn the main switch on and switch all individual circuits off. An ammeter in the positive line should not show any reading. If it indicates voltage, put the meter across individual circuits until the one at fault is found.

All shipboard ac wiring (for connection to an outlet ashore) should be completely independent of the dc wiring. It should also meet the standards for that used in homes ashore. The ac voltage is sufficient to be lethal—careful handling is essential. Shipboard alternating current (ac) wires are color-coded: black or red for the ungrounded conductor; white or transparent plastic for the current-carrying grounded conductor; and either green or bare wire for the grounded safety wire. The high voltage allows smaller diameter wires than those used for the low-voltage circuit.

The switchboard-to-shore cable should include a two-pole switch to break the circuit before any work is done on the system. Make sure that only built-in switches are wired in an ungrounded line. Equipment casings should be linked by a grounded safety wire to an underwater ground plate on the hull. This precaution will not affect the performance of components. Check the wiring to see that there are no breaks.

Most craft in American waters are wired for 115 volts with three-point receptacles. Larger craft, that require 230 volts, have four-point receptacles: there are two ungrounded wires and a neutral wire, as well as the noncurrent-carrying ground wire. There is 230 volts across the ungrounded wires, but between each and the neutral wire, 115 volts. Check through the wiring when making repairs if there is any doubt about what voltage is being used at any particular point.

The only electrical gear beyond owner regulation are the navigation lights. They have to comply with international and

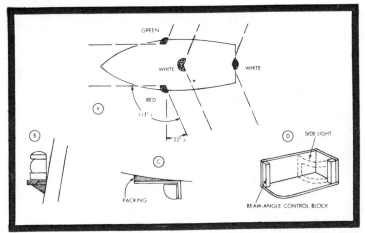

Fig. 8-6. The masthead light, port lights, and starboard lights should be adjusted for a 22½° beam (A). The lights can be mounted on shelves (B) and brackets (C). "Light boards" (D) are used to control the beam-angle of old oil burners.

other regulations. The regulations, however, don't specify that the lamps be electric. Oil lamps can be used, but seldom are. The correct arrangement of navigation lights is important for safety. Only when they are correctly aligned can anyone on another vessel be certain enough of your movements at night to take the correct action. Lamps should be adjusted within their housings to produce the correct beam angle for each. The white masthead light, the red port lights, and the green starboard lights should throw a beam from straight forward to "two points abaft the beam." The phrase dates from the days when compass points were used to describe directions. The angle is actually one-quarter of a right angle: 22½° (Fig. 8-6A). Electric navigation lights need not be so adjusted, provided they are properly mounted.

Lights on a sloping mast and side lights on a curved cabin must have their beams aimed correctly. A mast light should be upright on a shelf or bracket (Fig. 8-6B); side-light brackets may have to be packed from behind for proper aiming (Fig. 8-6C). Oil-burning side lights are often semi-enclosed in wooden structures, *light boards*, with blocks to cut off the beam to the correct angle (Fig. 8-6D). The stern light can't be adjusted for beam angle, but it may have to be supported like the masthead lights for beam direction.

# Appendixes

# Appendix A

# Galvanic Series of Metals

When two dissimilar metals are close together in salt water, the one towards the anodic end of the list will be eaten away; the further they are apart in the list, the more pronounced will be the effect.

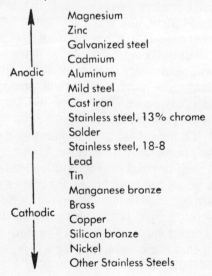

Anodic

Magnesium
Zinc
Galvanized steel
Cadmium
Aluminum
Mild steel
Cast iron
Stainless steel, 13% chrome
Solder
Stainless steel, 18-8
Lead
Tin
Manganese bronze
Brass
Copper
Silicon bronze
Nickel
Other Stainless Steels

Cathodic

# Appendix B
## Breaking Strengths of Rope

|               | \multicolumn{8}{c}{Diameter (in.)} |        |       |        |       |       |       |       |
| ------------- | ----- | ----- | ----- | ----- | ----- | ----- | ----- | ----- |
|               | $1/4$ | $5/16$ | $3/8$ | $7/16$ | $1/2$ | $9/16$ | $5/8$ | $3/4$ |
| Manilla       | 800   | 1200  | 1500  | 1950  | 2650  | 3450  | 4400  | 5400  |
| Nylon         | 1800  | 2900  | 4000  | 5400  | 7100  | 8900  | 11000 | 15000 |
| Polyester     | 1800  | 2900  | 3800  | 5200  | 6500  | 8300  | 10400 | 14400 |
| Polypropylene | 1250  | 1850  | 2600  | 3400  | 4150  | 4900  | 5900  | 7900  |
| Sisal         | 730   | 1000  | 1300  | 1700  | 2100  | 2800  | 3900  | 4500  |

# Appendix C
## Fid Sizes

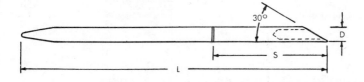

| Rope diam. |      | Fid diam. (D) | Fid length (L) | Short section (S) |
| ---------- | ---- | ------------- | -------------- | ----------------- |
| in.        | mm   | in.           | in.            | in.               |
| $1/4$      | 6    | $7/32$        | $5^1/2$        | $2^1/16$          |
| $5/16$     | 8    | $1/4$         | $6^3/4$        | $2^1/2$           |
| $3/8$      | 9    | $5/16$        | $7^3/4$        | $2^7/8$           |
| $7/16$     | 10   | $3/8$         | $9^1/2$        | $3^9/16$          |
| $1/2$      | 12   | $7/16$        | 11             | $4^1/8$           |
| $9/16$     | 14   | $1/2$         | $12^1/4$       | $3^5/8$           |
| $5/8$      | 16   | $9/16$        | 14             | $4^1/8$           |
| $3/4$      | 18   | $11/16$       | 16             | $4^3/4$           |
|            | 22   | $13/16$       | 19             | $4^3/4$           |
| 1          | 24   | $15/16$       | 21             | $5^1/4$           |

# Index